CARTOON★NATION presents
EST. 1776
U.S. IMMIGRATION

by Liam O'Donnell

illustrated by Charles Barnett III

CONSULTANT:

Michael Bailey
Colonel William J. Walsh Associate Professor
of American Government
Georgetown University, Washington, D.C.

Capstone
press

Mankato, Minnesota

Graphic Library is published by Capstone Press,
151 Good Counsel Drive, P.O. Box 669, Mankato, Minnesota 56002.
www.capstonepress.com

1 2 3 4 5 6 13 12 11 10 09 08

Library of Congress Cataloging-in-Publication Data
O'Donnell, Liam, 1970–
    U.S. immigration / by Liam O'Donnell; illustrated by Charles Barnett III.
    p. cm. — (Graphic library. Cartoon nation)
    Summary: "In cartoon format, explains the history of U.S. immigration and describes
how immigrants have shaped the United States" — Provided by publisher.
    Includes bibliographical references and index.
    ISBN-13: 978-1-4296-1983-7 (hardcover)
    ISBN-10: 1-4296-1983-X (hardcover)
    ISBN-13: 978-1-4296-2855-6 (softcover pbk.)
    ISBN-10: 1-4296-2855-3 (softcover pbk.)
    1. United States — Emigration and immigration — History — Juvenile literature. I.
Barnett, Charles, III, ill. II. Title. III. Series.
JV6450.O63 2009
304.8'73 — dc22   2008000488

Art Director and Designer
Bob Lentz

Production Designer
Kim Brown

Colorist
Krista Ward

Cover Artist
Kelly Brown

Editor
Christopher L. Harbo

TABLE OF CONTENTS

A COUNTRY BUILT BY IMMIGRATION

Do you know an immigrant? You probably do, and it may even be you! Immigrants are people who leave their home country to become part of another nation.

Now that might not be you, but it's probably true of your great-great-great grandparents. Most U.S. citizens are descendants of people who immigrated to America. That's why the United States is known as a nation of immigrants.

Pour in everything you can and this country will turn out great.

Sometimes, the United States is called a "melting pot." Many immigrants combine traditions from their old country with traditions from America.

descendant — a person's child and a family member born after that child

Of course, not everyone in the United States can trace their ancestors back to another country. Native Americans have ancestors who were here thousands of years before the United States became a nation.

ancestor — a family member who lived a long time ago

People have been moving from one country to another for thousands of years. Today, immigration happens all over the world. It makes countries stronger and better places to live.

Check out these muscles.

THE FIRST IMMIGRANTS

Some archaeologists believe the first people immigrated to North America 15,000 years ago. Others think the first immigrants arrived as far back as 40,000 years ago. Many believe they traveled across frozen land joining Siberia and Alaska. But others think the first immigrants arrived by boat along the western coastline.

The first immigrants to North America eventually became the Native American nations. For thousands of years, Native Americans lived in North America by themselves. They developed their own civilizations and languages.

Around AD 1000, the second group of immigrants arrived in North America. Vikings from Scandinavia sailed to the area known today as Newfoundland, Canada. They built settlements and made contact with some of the Native American tribes.

According to Viking sagas, the Vikings lived in Newfoundland for only about 10 years. Colder winters and diseases may have made life too difficult for the Vikings. Eventually, they decided to sail back to their homelands in Scandinavia.

saga — a long, detailed story; saga is the Viking word for "what is said."

EUROPE NOTICES NORTH AMERICA

The 1400s were a time of great exploration. Many ships sailed between European ports and Asia. At that time, the only way to get to Asia from Europe was to sail all the way around the southern coast of Africa.

AFRICA

I wish someone would discover a shortcut.

Spanish explorer Christopher Columbus wanted to find a faster way to Asia. In 1492, he sailed from Spain in his flagship, the Santa Maria. After two months at sea, he found land. Columbus believed he'd found a quicker route to Asia. He actually stumbled upon the Caribbean Islands off the southeast coast of North America.

I have arrived in Asia.

Don't tell him, but this is the Bahamas.

Columbus discovered the New World.

Amazing!

How can he discover it if people already live there?

Millions of Native Americans already lived in North America when Columbus arrived. Europeans didn't know North America existed until Columbus told them about it. They called North America the New World.

By the 1500s, Spanish adventurers, called conquistadors, arrived to explore North and South America. An African slave named Estevanico traveled with Spanish expeditions into the southwestern United States. Estevanico and the Spanish may have been the first non-Native Americans to enter the area now known as Arizona.

Let's go. There's sun, sand, and cactuses to explore.

You go ahead, Estevanico. We'll wait here until someone invents air conditioning.

GREEDY-FOR-GOLD

Columbus and other early explorers believed the land in North America was loaded with gold. They searched everywhere hoping to become rich. In reality, not much gold was found. But their greed caused these explorers to treat Native Americans with cruelty. They often killed them or took them as slaves.

EARLY SETTLERS

Soon Europeans poured into North America. In 1607, the first successful English settlement in America was founded in Jamestown, Virginia. It was founded on land controlled by the Powhatan Nation of Native Americans.

At first, the Powhatan gave gifts and traded food for copper items with the new immigrants. But Virginia was going through a drought. Soon the Powhatan could not grow enough food to meet the settlers' needs.

The settlers didn't know how to grow their own food. Starvation and disease spread quickly, killing many of them. Eventually they received help from Europe, and Jamestown flourished. Soon more settlements were established up and down the Atlantic coast.

Many of America's first immigrants were brought against their will as slaves. In the 1600s, slavery was legal. Ships brought people from Africa and the Caribbean to slave markets in North America. These people were sold as slaves to European immigrants. Today the descendants of many of those slaves are now U.S. citizens.

Meanwhile, Native Americans were unwelcome in their own country. They suffered greatly during the years of early immigration that created the United States. Through warfare and broken treaties, Native Americans had most of their land taken away. Much of their culture was destroyed.

THE PILGRIMS

The Pilgrims were some of the most famous immigrants to arrive in North America. They journeyed across the Atlantic from England in 1620. They had separated from the Church of England and wanted to practice their religion freely. They founded the Plymouth Colony in Massachusetts and are remembered for holding the very first Thanksgiving.

PASSING THROUGH ELLIS ISLAND

At the start of the 1900s, immigration to the United States was at its peak. People immigrated for different reasons. Many Irish and Italians came to escape the poverty of their home countries. Germans often immigrated to buy farmland in the Midwest.

Between 1892 and 1954, most people who immigrated to the United States entered through the same place: Ellis Island, New York.

At Ellis Island, immigrants were examined by U.S. Immigration officials and doctors. Doctors watched to see if people coughed, limped, or showed any other signs of sickness. The station was so busy, doctors only had a few seconds to check for cholera, tuberculosis, and other diseases.

You're healthy. Next!

cholera — a dangerous disease that causes severe sickness and diarrhea

Healthy people were allowed to leave the island and enter the United States. Sick people spent days or weeks in the medical wards on the island.

In the 62 years the immigration station was active, 12 million immigrants passed through Ellis Island. Only about 2 percent of immigrants trying to enter the United States were sent back to their home countries.

FAMOUS IMMIGRANTS

Of the millions of immigrants who passed through Ellis Island, some became famous:

BOB HOPE
ENTERTAINER;

CHARLIE CHAPLIN
ACTOR;

IRVING BERLIN
COMPOSER;

CHARLES ATLAS
BODY BUILDER;

CHALLENGES FOR IMMIGRANTS

Finding work was difficult for new immigrants. Many did not have the skills to work in the industrial jobs in America's cities. They worked as laborers building bridges and doing other dangerous jobs. In 1870, an unskilled laborer earned $1.75 for a 10-hour day of work. This amount was barely enough to buy food and pay rent.

Finding a safe place to live was another challenge. In 1900, most immigrants in New York lived in cramped apartments called tenements. These buildings were overcrowded and often filled with rats and other animals.

tenement — a rundown apartment building, especially one that is crowded and in a poor part of a city

To make life easier, immigrants joined together with others from their home country. In cities across America, Chinese immigrants created safe places, called Chinatowns, to practice their cultural traditions. An organization called the Order of the Sons of Italy helped immigrants arriving from Italy.

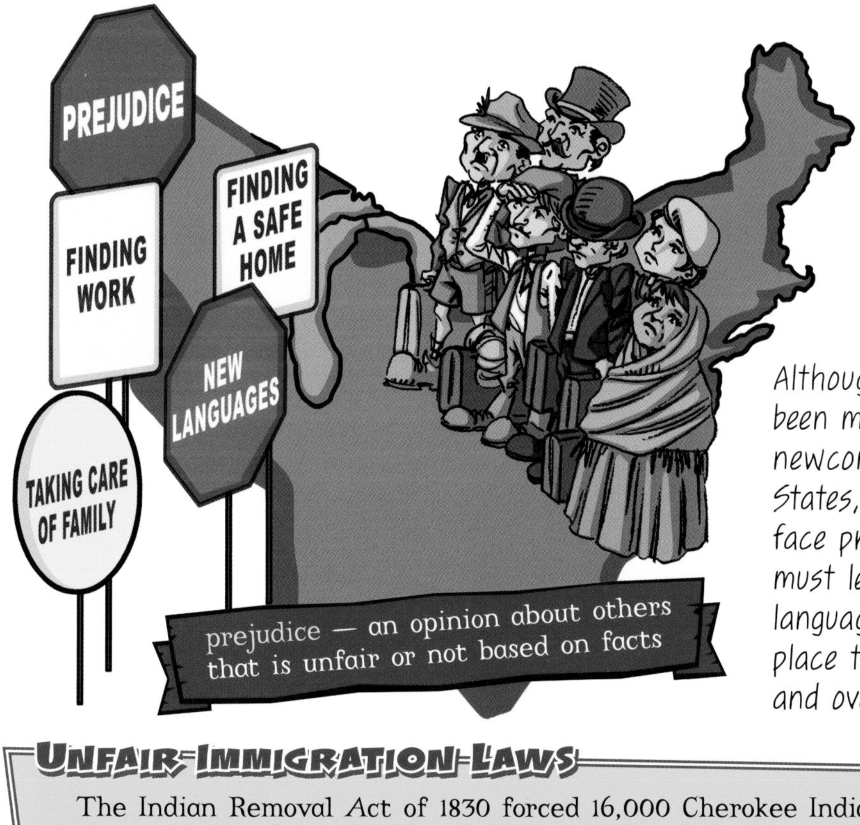

PREJUDICE

FINDING WORK

FINDING A SAFE HOME

NEW LANGUAGES

TAKING CARE OF FAMILY

Although laws have been made to protect newcomers to the United States, immigrants still face problems. They must learn a new language, find a safe place to live and work, and overcome prejudice.

prejudice — an opinion about others that is unfair or not based on facts

Unfair Immigration Laws

The Indian Removal Act of 1830 forced 16,000 Cherokee Indians to relocate west of the Mississippi River. Cherokees were forced to march 1,000 miles to their new territory. At least 4,000 Cherokees died on the march, now known as the Trail of Tears.

The Chinese Exclusion Act of 1882 banned Chinese laborers from entering the United States. This law also forbid Chinese immigrants living in the United States from becoming citizens. The law was overturned 61 years later, but there were still limits on Chinese immigration until 1965.

Today, people who want to immigrate to the United States must first apply for permission.

This process begins at the U.S. Embassy in their home country. Many forms need to be filled out. Processing the application can take many months.

embassy — a building where representatives from another country work

Successful applicants receive a document called a visa. This permission slip allows them to come to the United States to live and work. The document is a green-colored card and is commonly known as a "green card." A green card must be renewed every 10 years.

"Green card" – original name, huh?

People with green cards are called lawful permanent residents. They are allowed to live and work in the United States, but they are not yet U.S. citizens. Lawful permanent residents cannot vote in elections or hold public office.

What are you doing?

I'm going to be a citizen soon, so I'm practicing how to hold public office.

Lawful permanent residents can apply to have their husband, wife, and unmarried children immigrate to the United States. People who put a large sum of money into an American business can get an investor visa. This visa will let them immigrate to the United States.

Right this way, Mr. Investor.

The rest of you must wait your turn.

THE LOTTERY

Each year in the United States, 55,000 green cards are up for grabs in the Diversity Visa Lottery Program. Lottery winners get a chance to become lawful permanent residents.

WHY PEOPLE IMMIGRATE

People immigrate for many reasons. Some leave their home country to live with family. Others immigrate because they can find a better job in their new country. For others, immigrating is a chance to make a better life for themselves and their family.

In some countries, many people live in poverty because jobs are difficult to find. Some choose to leave their country in search of work. This trend is called the "push factor," because it is like the people are being pushed out of their home country.

Wealthy countries like the United States have plenty of jobs that need workers. But many U.S. citizens won't take these jobs because they don't pay enough or they are too dangerous.

Hi, we're here for jobs.

Great! We've got openings for gardeners, sanitation workers, or nannies.

Um, any openings for pop stars or professional basketball players?

JOB CENTER

Immigrants are willing to take these jobs because they can often earn more than they would in their home country. This trend is called the "pull factor" because it is like the jobs pull people to richer countries.

War, famine, or political struggles can put people's lives in danger and force them to immigrate. People who try to immigrate to a new country because their lives are in danger are called asylum seekers. If they are allowed to immigrate into the new country, they become refugees.

refugee — a person forced to flee his or her home because of natural disaster or war

19

UNDOCUMENTED IMMIGRANTS

For some people, the push factor in their home country is very strong. They will risk their lives to immigrate to a new country without permission.

THE PUSH FACTOR DILEMMA

OBEY THE LAW AND YOUR FAMILY GOES HUNGRY.

BREAK THE LAW AND FEED YOUR FAMILY.

Immigrating without permission is against the law. These people are often called illegal immigrants. They are also called undocumented immigrants because they don't have proper immigration documents like a green card.

Your green card is almost expired.

I'm on my way to get it renewed!

Immigrants can also become undocumented if they stay in the country after their visas expire.

A common way for undocumented immigrants to enter the United States is to cross the border with Mexico. Most of this border runs through desert and is very dangerous to cross on foot. Each year, hundreds of people die from harsh desert conditions while trying to cross the border.

The U.S. government built tall fences along parts of the border between Mexico and the United States. The fences are meant to stop people from coming into the United States illegally. Guards patrol the U.S. border and try to stop people from crossing into the country illegally.

REMOVAL

If people who enter the United States illegally are caught, they are taken out of the country. Sending people back used to be called deportation, but now the U.S. government calls it removal.

BECOMING A CITIZEN

Becoming citizens of their new country is the goal for many immigrants. In 2006, more than 700,000 people became U.S. citizens.

Congratulations! You are now all U.S. citizens.

The process of becoming a U.S. citizen is called naturalization. U.S. citizenship allows immigrants to vote in elections, serve on a jury in a court trial, and hold political office.

To become citizens, permanent residents must have lived in the United States for at least five years. They must be able to read, write, and speak English. They must also agree to follow the laws of the United States.

Sir, you arrived in the United States yesterday. You can't apply for citizenship for another four years and 364 days.

That's okay. I'll wait here.

Potential citizens must also know United States history and how the U.S. government works. And they have to pass a test to prove it.

I'm so nervous I forgot how to spell U.S.A.

The naturalization test is made up of 10 questions about U.S. history and government. A person needs to get six questions right to pass the test and become a U.S. citizen.

TEST YOUR KNOWLEDGE

The U.S. citizenship test has a variety of questions about U.S. history, government, and politics. Here are a few sample questions to test your knowledge:

1. Why are there 100 senators in the United States Senate?

2. What is the executive of a state government called?

3. When was the Declaration of Independence adopted?

4. Name some countries that were our enemies during World War II.

1. Each state elects two senators; 2. Governor; 3. July 4, 1776; 4. Germany, Italy, and Japan

BENEFITS OF IMMIGRATION

The United States was built by the hard work of immigrants from around the world. It still is today. Look around and you will see the benefits of immigration.

In 2006, the U.S. government did a study on immigration. It found that legal immigration is good for the country's economy.

The report said that the U.S. economy creates more jobs than can be filled by U.S. citizens. Immigrants fill these jobs and help the United States be more productive. They make the country wealthier and improve living conditions for many Americans.

Immigrants also help the U.S. government and businesses get along with other countries. They can teach the government and businesses about traditions and opportunities in their home countries. Immigrants help the United States trade with countries around the world.

It's a deal!

U.S.A.

JAPAN

But immigrants bring more than political and economic benefits to the United States. If you like pizza, burritos, rice, or falafel, then you've tasted the benefits of immigration. These foods, and many others, were first brought to America by immigrants to the United States. See how many other immigration influences you can find in your home, school, or neighborhood.

Mmm, immigration tastes delicious!

HIGH-TECH IMMIGRANTS

Immigrants are responsible for creating many high-tech businesses, such as Google and Sun Microsystems. Sabeer Bhatia, from India, invented an e-mail program called Hotmail. He later sold it to Microsoft for a reported $400 million.

As long as there are push and pull factors in the world, people will immigrate to new countries. They will continue to search for a place to live a better life.

Many immigrants try to eliminate the push factors of poverty by investing money in their home countries. Some Mexican migrant workers send money they've earned in the United States to home associations in their home country.

The associations use the money to pave roads, invest in factories, build churches, and more. These projects create jobs and reduce poverty in Mexican communities.

Whether they realize it or not, American citizens rely on immigrants every day. Everything from the clothes people wear to the food they eat is made possible because of the hard work of immigrants. These workers were pulled to the United States because of the need for people to fill jobs.

CELL PHONE: DESIGNED, SOLD, AND SERVICED BY U.S. IMMIGRANTS

COFFEE: BREWED AND SERVED BY U.S. IMMIGRANTS

GROCERIES: MADE, SHIPPED, AND SOLD BY U.S. IMMIGRANTS

FRUITS AND VEGETABLES: GROWN, PICKED, AND PACKED BY U.S. IMMIGRANTS

CLOTHES: DESIGNED AND SOLD BY U.S. IMMIGRANTS

The United States is a nation of immigrants. It will continue to welcome others who want to join the melting pot of America.

WELCOME

TIME LINE

40,000–15,000 BC — The very first immigrants arrive in North America. They spread out over the entire continent to create the Native American nations.

AD 1000 — The Vikings land in present-day Newfoundland, Canada. They make contact with the Inuit people living in the area.

AD 1000

40,000–15,000 BC

1882 — The Chinese Exclusion Act of 1882 bans Chinese laborers from entering the United States. It also prevents Chinese immigrants living in the United States from becoming citizens. The law stays in effect for more than 60 years.

1620 — The Pilgrims arrive from England and create the Plymouth Colony in Massachusetts.

1620

1892 — Ellis Island Immigration Station opens to process the thousands of European immigrants arriving to the U.S. each year. More than 12 million immigrants pass through Ellis Island during its 62 years of operation.

1882

1892

ELLIS ISLAND

1492 — Christopher Columbus arrives in North America. Europeans begin pouring into the New World and settling the Native Americans' lands.

1492

1607 — The first successful English settlement in America is founded in Jamestown, Virginia.

JAMESTOWN

1607

1619 — The first African slaves arrive in Jamestown, Virginia. For more than 200 years, slave ships continue to bring African slaves to America.

1619

1952 — The Immigration and Nationality Act is passed. It allows people of all races to become citizens.

2006 — The Secure Fence Act of 2006 is passed. The act allows for 700 miles of fence to be built along the border between Mexico and the United States. The fence is meant to slow the number of illegal immigrants crossing into the United States.

2006

1952

GLOSSARY

ancestor (AN-sess-tur) — a family member who lived a long time ago

cholera (KOL-ur-uh) — a dangerous disease that causes severe sickness and diarrhea

civilization (si-vuh-luh-ZAY-shuhn) — an organized and advanced society

conquistador (kon-KEYS-tuh-dor) — a leader in the Spanish conquest of North and South America during the 1500s

descendant (di-SEN-duhnt) — a person's child and a family member born after that child

embassy (EM-buh-see) — a building where representatives from another country work

naturalization (nach-ur-uh-luh-ZAY-shuhn) — the process of giving citizenship to someone who was born in another country

prejudice (PREJ-uh-diss) — an opinion about others that is unfair or not based on facts

refugee (ref-yuh-JEE) — a person forced to flee his or her home because of natural disaster or war

saga (SAH-gah) — a long, detailed story; saga is the Viking word for "what is said."

tenement (TEN-uh-muhnt) — a rundown apartment building, especially one that is crowded and in a poor part of a city

tuberculosis (tu-BUR-kyoo-low-sis) — a disease caused by bacteria that causes fever, weight loss, and coughing

visa (VEE-zuh) — a document giving a person permission to enter a foreign country

READ MORE

Britton, Tamara L. *Ellis Island.* Symbols, Landmarks, and Monuments. Edina, Minn.: ABDO, 2004.

Hanel, Rachael. *Mexican Immigrants in America: An Interactive History Adventure.* You Choose Books. Mankato, Minn.: Capstone Press, 2009.

Skog, Jason. *Citizenship.* Cartoon Nation. Mankato, Minn.: Capstone Press, 2008.

Teichmann, Iris. *Life as an Immigrant.* Understanding Immigration. North Mankato, Minn.: Smart Apple Media, 2007.

Wilson, Ruth. *Immigration: A Look at the Way the World Is Today.* Issues of the World. Mankato, Minn.: Stargazer Books, 2006.

INTERNET SITES

FactHound offers a safe, fun way to find Internet sites related to this book. All of the sites on FactHound have been researched by our staff.

Here's how:
1. Visit *www.facthound.com*
2. Choose your grade level.
3. Type in this book ID 142961983X for age-appropriate sites. You may also browse subjects by clicking on letters, or by clicking on pictures and words.
4. Click on the Fetch It button.

FactHound will fetch the best sites for you!

INDEX

Penny Pollard's Passport

Robin Klein
Illustrated by Ann James

Melbourne
Oxford University Press
Oxford Auckland New York

Kooringa Supersave Hypermart
Kooringa Mall
KOORINGA   30567

Alistair Ross
35 Marks Street
KOORINGA 30567

Dear Alistair Ross

With regard to our recent travel competition in which you were the owner of the winning ticket (although we didn't know that you are only 12 years old): As you know, the prize is a bus tour of the United Kingdom for TWO ADULTS. However, as you've correctly pointed out, there were no stipulations in the conditions of entry regarding age.

We really cannot agree to your alternative suggestion that we allow two children to travel instead, as we feel that it would be undesirable for minors, no matter how sensible, to travel alone overseas without adult super-vision.

However, as Kooringa Supersave Hypermart's policy has always been to please the customer, we will adjust the first prize and allow one adult fare and two child fares.

Hi-Fli Tours, our co-sponsors, will be in touch with your mother regarding the airline bookings, itinerary details of the coach tour, and your London hotel reservations for the start and finish of the tour.

Heartiest congratulations, and we hope that you and your two lucky travelling companions have a very pleasant time.

Thank you for shopping at Kooringa Supersave Hypermart.

Yours sincerely

Dennis Coghlan
Manager

Dear Alistair

Wow! Have you got your passport yet? Mine looks *ace*, though Mum wouldn't let me wear my camouflage sniper jacket for the photo. She said I might get arrested as a terrorist. Whew! Am I glad that passport finally turned up in time. (There was a bit of a muck up over the application form and it had to be done again.)

You can't believe all the lectures I've been getting from Mum and Dad about how I've got to behave in the U.K. and not give Australia a bad name. Mum rang school to see if it was okay to take time off and Miss James said yes (probably glad to get rid of me for a couple of weeks) but she's set this assignment I've got to do on 'Three Important Historical Sites in England' only she reckons the Loch Ness Monster can't be one of them. Al, are you really *sure* it's okay for me to come along? What about your mum, are you *positive* she didn't make any objections? (Because let's face it, she doesn't like me all that much.)

Got to keep pinching myself to really believe it. I've never been further than Adelaide before!

See ya at the *International* airport.

Penny

THINGS TO PACK (NON-URGENT)
- one pair spare jeans
- tracksuit (can double as PJ's, dressing-gown, extra clothes, etc.)
- spare pair undies (or get paper ones, less trouble, no washing)
- one T-shirt
- Red-back spider windcheater
- one pair spare socks (camouflage ones so don't show dirt)
- beaut camouflage army sniper jacket
- judo pants with embroidered ants (if you're the ants pants you may as well wear them)
- book to do miss J.'s daggy assignments in.

pie bag emperor gum moth cocoon   gum leaves   eucalyptus oil   goanna oil linament

VITAL! URGENT! NOT TO BE LEFT BEHIND ON ANY ACCOUNT!

Billy,

fly swat
cockatoo feathers

Swap card collection, camera, writing stuff, type-
writer, two large jars VEGEMITE, compass, chart
with different times around the world, bathers,
airsick tablets, Barley Sugar, address book, mouth
organ, khaki knapsack with camouflage pockets,
library books about English ghosts and Loch Ness
monster, snacks, things to do on plane, photo of
Bill, glove puppets - kookaburra and cockatoo - to
double as mittens on cold days and souvenirs of
Australia to give away, other souvenirs, air force boots.

Penny, I've repacked for you properly. Madam,
and don't you dare add or subtract anything
to the following in your suitcase:
SIX pairs undies
SIX pairs socks
DECENT pyjamas
PROPER dressing gown
GOOD jeans
ENOUGH clean shirts
RESPECTABLE jacket
ONE DRESS (not to be lost anywhere en route!)
RESPECTABLE shoes
NEW pullover

PLUS cap, gloves, toothbrush, toothpaste, nail file,
paper tissues, comb. You are DEFINITELY NOT ALLOWED
to take that tacky khaki knapsack - it smells of
sump oil. Transfer all small articles to the nice
plastic carry bag provided by Hi-Fli Tours. Passport and traveller's cheques to be given to Mrs Ross
for safe keeping, NOT pinned inside that ridiculous
money belt you made out of old purses, buckles
and scarves. (Who do you think you are, Al Capone?)

Mum

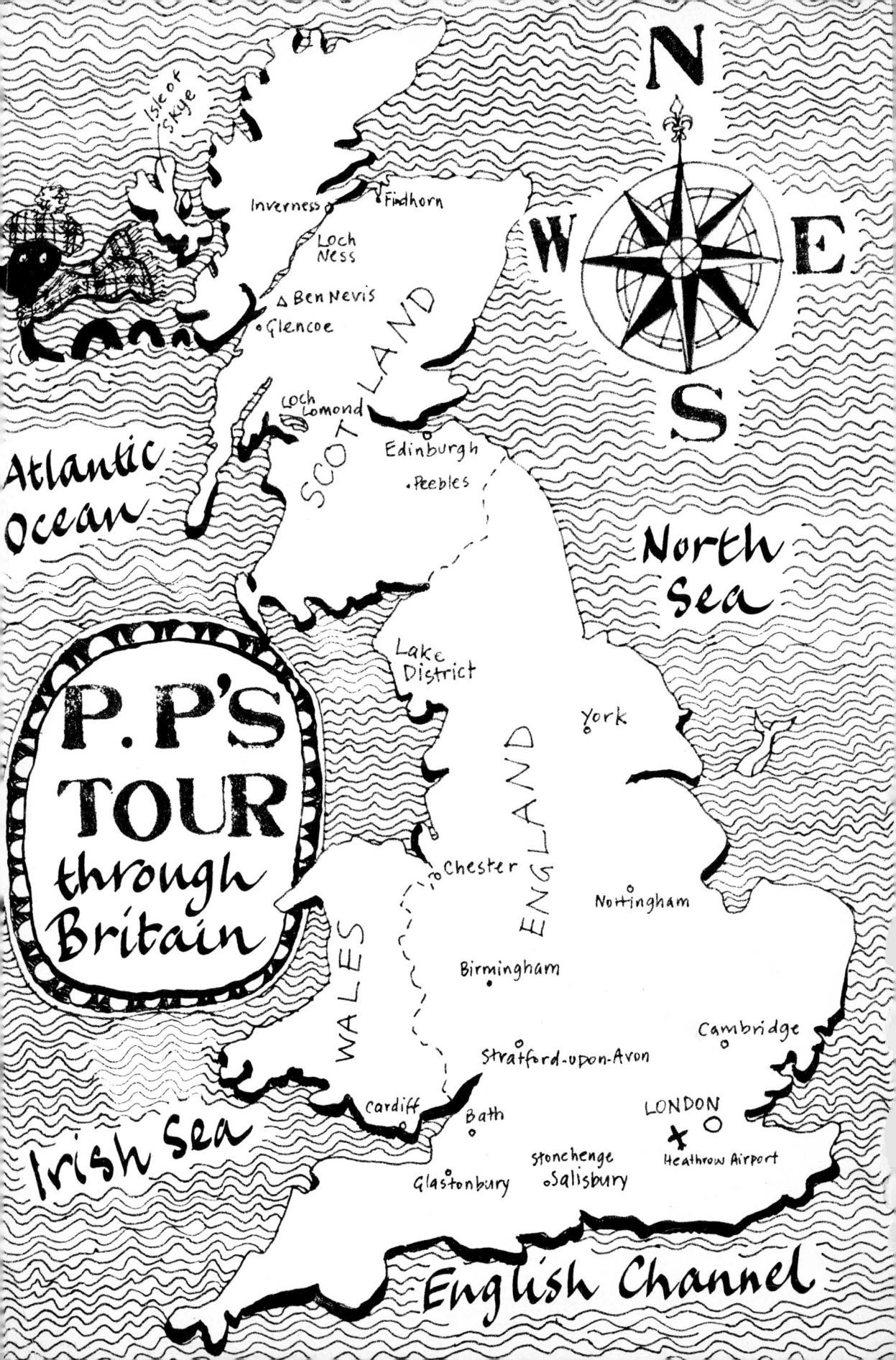

Please fold out for map of Britain

↓

Dear Penny,

Don't let on to Mum, but here's some extra pocket money for the trip. I know we all agreed on a fixed budget for you, but it's not every day you get the chance to be a member of the Jet set.

Go for it, gal!

Love
Dad

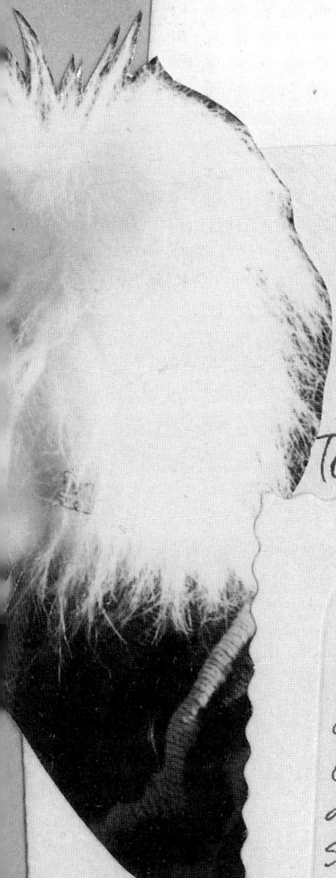

To Be Opened on the Plane

Dear Penny,

Have a lovely time, darling! You can change these notes at Heathrow Airport. (No need to mention it to Dad, he was so insistent about the budget, but this is a little extra something from me, anyhow.) Don't spend it all on badges.

Love,
Mum

P.S. Do try to stay out of trouble, Penny!

London

Dear Mum and Dad

Thanks *a heap* for the beaut surprise letters which I opened on the plane! We got here okay and I let Alistair have the window seat most of the time like you said. (Though it was kind of wasted on him: all he did was read a book about politics.)

You said I'd packed too much to take on the plane, but you should have seen what Mrs Ross had in her Hi-Fli tour bag: moisture cream so her skin wouldn't dry out, neck pillow so she wouldn't get whiplash, special foot pillow to stop her feet swelling, ear plugs, and a Lone Ranger eye mask.

There was this girl a bit younger than Alistair and me sitting in the aisle across from us. She was with her mum. They're booked on the same bus tour as us, only Heidi (that's her name) said they're *paying* for *their* trip, not like us winning it as a prize. She's a bit stuck up and I didn't like her mum much, either. (All she did was chain smoke and give herself a manicure from Melbourne to when we flew over the Austrian Alps and then she had a sleep and told Heidi she wasn't allowed to make any noise or fidget.)

Over the Austrian Alps they came and closed all the blinds even though the sun was coming up. People went back to sleep, but I was too excited about getting closer by the minute to seeing the Loch Ness Monster. I asked the steward how long before we landed and he said: 'Half an hour'. So I shook Mrs Ross and Alistair awake and we got all our stuff out of the overhead lockers and Mrs Ross put on a new lot of make-up. But then the steward came back and looked surprised we weren't asleep like everyone else. It turned out what he'd said was '*five-and-a-half-hours*' (!) but I hadn't heard him properly. Mrs Ross wasn't very pleased.

It was *beaut* flying down over London and seeing all the two-storey houses like dolls' houses, and really exciting going through Customs because there were hundreds of different nationalities and people wearing saris and Arabian tea-towel hats. (I was glad I was wearing my cap with the crocheted yabby on top I made in craft though you said it looks daggy, because I felt I was representing Australia in that long queue.) Landing in England was like a 200-year-old link with great-great-grandfather because he was a convict (even though Aunt Winifred still says he was actually the chaplain on the convict ship and didn't believe all those photocopies Dad got from Trace-Your-Ancestry).

When we finally got through Customs, Mrs Ross and Alistair were a bit jet-lagged, so I found a taxi for us and told the driver where to go, which was the Tower of London, as I thought the other two would want to see that first thing and not waste a minute. But Mrs Ross redirected him straight to the hotel. She said we'd all have to have a good rest to be ready for the bus tour tomorrow and we'd have the chance to see London when we got back from that. I pointed out I'd already had a long sleep on the plane and she said a bit snappily she wished she could say the same, but when she finally dropped off a certain person had woken her up over the Austrian Alps with misleading information.

Our hotel is great (except that Heidi is in the next room). They don't have proper showers, only a hose you unhook, but there are these terrific heated racks you dry towels on. I washed my hair (accident with container of apple cider on the plane, it's not a good idea to stab them open with a fork) and that heated towel rack is really handy for drying hair, too, though you get a cricked neck. It wasn't even lunch time yet, but Mrs Ross made me get into bed and go back to sleep.

The view from the hotel window is terrific, red double-decker buses going by and lots of punks hanging round the corner, though Mrs Ross is very disappointed and said she thought it would be a first-class hotel like it said in the Hi-Fli brochure. (Alistair said he wouldn't stay in a first class hotel on principal because working-class people could never afford them.) I don't mind that the room shakes a bit with traffic and knobs keep falling off the telly, but it's hard watching those red buses go by down in the street with me not on one of them. I'm remembering what you said about not nicking off on my own, so I guess I'll just have to stay put here in bed until Mrs Ross and Alistair get over their jet lag. Heidi reckons she *never* gets jet lag and she's been overseas six times, but when I went for a walk along the corridor, their door was open and she was fast asleep snoring her head off.

More later, give Bill a big hug from me,

Love,
penny   X X
              X

This is what the red double-decker buses look like Bill. I'll bring one back for you. (a toy one I mean).

Dear Mrs Bettany

Well, they let me into the U.K. even though Jason Taylor said they never would once they got an eyeful of my passport photo.

Today we set off on our bus tour, only we were a bit late because I accidentally got my foot stuck in a shoe-cleaning machine in the hotel foyer and they had to call the hotel mechanic to prise the rollers apart. (I'm not all that sure it was accidental. There's this kid Heidi travelling on the same tour as us, and she sort of pushed all the buttons at the one time. She said she'd only been trying to help, but I know a gloat when I see one.)

There are a lot of people travelling on this bus, including two very nice Chinese, some Canadians and Americans and the rest from New Zealand and Australia. The driver's name is Jeffrey and the tour leader Gus. (They look a bit shifty, so Alistair and I call them The Dodgy Brothers though not to their faces.) Before we even got started they announced how much passengers usually tip them at the end of each tour. Alistair said that Hi-Fli Tours should pay them proper salaries so they don't have to rely on tips, and Gus gave him a very dirty look.

One of the Americans was sitting behind me and he said his name was Barb. I guess it's short for Barber, which seems a very weird first name, but there are two other Americans called Milton and Candy, so maybe they go in for unusual names in the U.S.A. Barb looks a bit lonely because he's travelling all by himself, but there's another lady travelling alone, too, Lucy Bryson. She was on the plane coming over and she's really nice and writes romance novels. She's looking forward to seeing Scotland so she can get ideas for a book she's writing called *Love Amid The Heather*. (She let me read some of it on the plane, and it's a bit soppy.)

Heidi is too stuck up to talk to Alistair and me. She sits down the back of the bus by herself and carries on about how cold it is, even though she's got a blue mesh travel rug. (It looks a bit like the ones the airline lent people for sleeping.)

Cambridge was our first stop and the itinerary said we'd be taken on a guided tour of the university colleges, but Gus announced that he'd just found out guided tours weren't allowed today because of exams, so we'd have to walk around on our own for an hour. Everyone headed off for a famous church called King's College Chapel which is all white and lacy like being inside a giant pavlova. We all looked up at the ceiling with holy expressions as though we were film extras in *Close Encounters of the Third Kind*, and said it was so beautiful we could stand there gazing at it for ever. After a couple of minutes we all started rubbing our necks and saying ouch, so we went out to look at the shops.)

Alistair bought a mouldy old book printed in 1935 all about trade unions and I bought this fantastic furry busby. It's made of real bearskin with a wicker frame and I'm going to give it to Dad. Then we walked for a long time trying to find students punting on the river, which Mrs Ross said was a well-known Cambridge tourist sight she'd often read about and wanted to photograph, but all the boats were tied up and empty. She asked someone going by where all the students were and he shrugged and said probably in the pubs drinking. Mrs Ross looked very annoyed and it didn't help any that she collected a clout across the shins from my walking stick and laddered her pantyhose.

Alistair had his nose stuck in his new book, so I moved back and got chatting with Barb, and guess what! He has a *ranch* in *Texas*! He said it hasn't got any oil wells on it and it's only small like a hobby farm, and he can't ride and doesn't own a Stetson hat, either, but I felt very honoured sitting next to a real Texas rancher. I gave him a free gift souvenir of Australia, which was a Sydney Opera House pencil eraser and he gave me a key-ring which is a plastic map outline of Texas.

I hope you like this postcard of a thatched cottage, which I bought at a little village of them where we stopped for lunch after we visited Cambridge.

love,
Penny
x

I might invent
a new 'thatch-look'
haircut with scallops
at the top.

Alistair,
I wish you'd get your nose out of that book. Just have a listen occasionally to that Heidi Denver. She keeps running down Australia and giving it a bad name to everyone from other countries on the bus. She told Candy and Milton and Mrs Chong it's very boring and you have to carry a can of flyspray everywhere you go.
She thinks she's so great with all that pocket money. Did you see the masses of stuff she bought in Cambridge? How about I move down to the backseat and practise some judo strangleholds?
P.

Dear Uncle Dave

This is a postcard of Sherwood Forest, only there's hardly any of it left. It doesn't look as though it could have ever been big enough to hide even one merry man, let along a whole gang.* We stopped at a place called the Maid Marian Tea Rooms and were late getting on the road again, because a lady called Lucy Bryson wandered off to take a photo of an oak tree (in case Robin Hood had climbed it) and got bailed up by a spotty cow who'd never heard about international relationships. Barb (my new friend from Texas, U.S.A.) climbed through the fence and rescued her, just like a knight in shining armour.

See ya,
Penny

*I saw a police car with Nottinghamshire Constabulary on it. I bet the Sheriff of Nottingham would have liked something zappy like that to catch up with Robin Hood.

bailed up Lucy Bryson
– gallantly rescued by Barb
It's a stone fence
(probably fossilised)

(I think he looks a bit shifty.)

The Sheriff of Nottingham →
(today's)

hood COUNTRY

Ollerton
Edwinstowe   Major Oak   Wellow
Hunting Lodge   Maypole
Clipstone   Friar Tuck   Newark Castle
Mansfield
A 617
Newstead Abbey   Fountaindale   SHERWOOD FOREST   Southwell   NEWARK
Friar Tucks'   Minster
Well
Robin Hoods
Stables
Papplewick   Nottingham
Castle
Hucknall   NOTTINGHAM

11

DIARY

Lucy's not all that old, probably about the same age as Mrs Ross and Mum. She looks lonely. She must get sick of having to sit next to Mrs Ross in the bus all the time and hear about how brainy Alistair is at school. It suddenly hit me that maybe she might like a real-life romance of her own instead of just writing about them. I thought if I could get her sitting next to Barb, he'd find out how nice she is, only my plan didn't work all that well. I told Mrs R. I was feeling bus sick and could I sit next to her because Alistair kept spreading his maps of the British Isles all over the seat and I might chunder into them. Mrs Ross told me not to talk as though I wore thongs, shorts and a singlet with an ad for beer on it, but she let me sit next to her with an open plastic bag just in case.

It was all a waste of time. Lucy didn't move into the empty seat next to Barb like I thought she would. Instead she went right down the back and Heidi started showing her all these little woolly toy lambs she got at the Maid Marian Tea Rooms souvenir shop. Heidi has enough of them to start a sheep farm.

We came to an ace city called York where Guy Fawkes was born. We were supposed to have a guided historical tour there, but Gus said it was a misprint in the itinerary and York was where they always had the bus serviced. So everyone just went off sight-seeing by themselves for an hour. Heidi came tagging after me and Alistair and said she'd lost her mum in the crowd, which I suspect she did on purpose. (Can't say I really blame her.)

The first place we looked at was York Cathedral. It was old. Mrs Ross made us sit down and listen to a choir practice going on, though Alistair said he got quite enough of that at school, and then we went and looked at the shops. They were fantastic, in narrow bendy streets with the roofs nearly meeting in the middle. Mrs R. said they used to be houses in olden times. It must have been quite handy living like that. You could have borrowed a cup of barley or a spare candle just by reaching across the street through an upstairs window. (Though I could think of some people I wouldn't want to have as neighbours if you had to live like that now — Simone Norris, for one. She'd be forever reaching over the road and thumping on your window to show off the pink ballet dress she'd made for her latest Cabbage Patch Kid.)

I bought a little pottery cottage for Auntie Sue. Heidi reckoned it was exactly the sort of thing tourists *always* buy. (What a hypocrite! I noticed her coat pockets were stuffed full of little souvenirs just like that little cottage, and she'd been in such a rush to buy them she apparently hadn't bothered asking the shop assistants to wrap them up, either.)

choir boys after practice - I think they're going off to play pool

Mrs Ross wanted to look in antique shops, so she let Alistair and me climb the old city walls. It was fantastic up there, even though Heidi trailed along and we couldn't get rid of her. I took a photo through a real arrow slit into someone's oak-tree garden. Heidi said tourists always take photos of gardens in England. She said she'd already been to England once before with her dad and she doesn't think its such a big deal and New York is better, even though it's pretty boring too like everywhere else specially Bali. She said she sometimes lives with her dad and her stepmother and sometimes with her mum in between divorces and they all take her on trips and she's been all over the world.

I was just about fed up to my crocheted yabby with Heidi and her skiting so I said I bet she'd never been to Ming Chu. Heidi boasted she was going there on a chartered flight on her next birthday and her dad had already made the bookings. I said the pilot might have trouble landing, seeing Ming Chu is the name of the Chinese take-away café in the Kooringa shopping mall back home.

We met someone else from our bus tour up on the old city walls. His name is Dudley Fowler and he's very short and a bit boring with not much hair. So while he was droning on to Alistair about filters and short angle lenses, I thought I'd like to go for a walk right around the walls, only I didn't know if there'd be time before the bus left. Heidi asked me why I didn't have a watch. I certainly didn't want to tell her about making a loaf of chilli-flavoured bread to surprise Mum and my watch slipped off while I was kneading the dough and got baked. So I just said I couldn't wear watches because they always stopped mysteriously like that man on TV who has peculiar powers.

14

Heidi pulled up her sleeve and she was wearing *two* watches, a digital one and a new looking Micky Mouse one. (Wearing two watches at the same time is about the highest form of showing off you can get!) But Heidi offered to stand right there where she could see our bus parked and as soon as people started to head back to it, she promised to wave to me as a signal. So I took off round the wall, thinking maybe I'd misjudged her and she wasn't such the little fink I had imagined.

It was totally magnificent walking along those old walls pretending to be a Roman soldier on sentry duty, but after a bit I looked back and Heidi had vanished mysteriously. I shot down the nearest flight of steps thinking I'd better take a short cut back to the bus if I didn't want to be left behind and have to live in York permanently not knowing anyone, only it turned out to be a longer short cut than I thought. When I got back, Gus said angrily that everyone had been looking all over the place for me and I'd held the tour schedule up by twenty-five minutes. I glared at Heidi who was sitting up the back winding her new Micky Mouse watch and looking as innocent as a murderer in an Agatha Christie book. She didn't own up that it had been her fault, so I said I'd just been asking people directions to the loo but couldn't understand their Yorkshire accents and I'd ended up in a corn market instead.

Gus wouldn't stop for any more photos along the way because I'd held up the schedule, but it didn't matter because everyone was falling asleep from the long day and too much sight-seeing crammed into it. Just when we'd all got nicely settled and snoozing, Gus woke us up by putting on a tape of 'The Happy Wanderer' with the sound turned up full blast. He made everyone join in the choruses until we got to the hotel where we were booked for the first night of our tour.

Mrs Ross said I had to get smartened up for dinner now that we were in a civilized, cultured country like England. So I put on my red-back spider wind-cheater, my judo ants pants and my airforce boots, but Mrs Ross made me change into the dress Mum had packed. (Alistair was just as badly off. She made him wear a tie, even though he muttered all the way down in the lift about Human Rights and the Geneva Convention.)

I wasn't quick enough to steer Lucy into the vacant chair next to Barb. Heidi's mum got there first, so poor Lucy ended up sitting next to that boring Dudley Fowler from Nullagumana on the Murray River, and he didn't say one word all through dinner!

York Cathedral (make a good wedding-cake design for Royalty)

neat spyhole int someone's ga (I wish I'd ga a bow and a to practi

A scot doing the Highland fling

Dear Aunty Janice

I've just been to a Scottish wool mill. You should have seen all the kilts! If I'd had enough money I would have got one for Uncle Brian so he could show off his hairy legs. Everyone from our bus went crazy when they saw all those kilts and they all suddenly remembered they had Scotch ancestors (or at least that's what they claimed) and were entitled to wear tartan. Mrs Ross went one better and said *she* was related to the Scottish monarchs and bought herself a Royal Stewart kilt with a beret and scarf to match and a Royal Stewart tie for Alistair, though I reckon it will make him look like a box of Highland toffee.

I bought a tie with a stag's head on it for Uncle Brian and while I was at the counter I found this man called Barber Ziegenhagen from Texas who's on our bus, too, looking a bit sad because he hadn't been able to think of any Scottish ancestry in his family at all. I asked the girl behind the counter if they had a tartan anyone could wear even if they didn't belong to a clan, and they did, so Barb brightened up and bought a whole lot of ties for his nephews back in Dallas.

There's this lady on the bus, Lucy Bryson (she's not from Texas, she's from Melbourne) and she was going to buy a daggy grey skirt and jacket to match. But I talked her into buying this zingy kilt instead, all zappy yellow, scarlet and orange checks. (Just seeing it makes you want to get up and dance a Highland Fling.)

Everyone staggered back to the bus loaded down with tartan car rugs, scarves, kilts, thistle-shaped kilt pins, ties, hairy socks, tartan caps with pom poms etc. The only person who didn't buy anything was Alistair. He reckons impulsive souvenir-buying is a serious mental disease and he'd heard it gets worse towards the end of any tour and by then nobody wants to go into cathedrals or historical places, they just dive frantically off their bus into souvenir shops instead, punching each other in the rush to be first. He says it's a good example of how unhealthy capitalist societies are. (I felt a bit guilty showing him the sporran I bought on impulse in case I ever decide to change my name to Penny MacPollard.)

Lucy showed her kilt to Mrs Ross and Mrs Ross put on her sunglasses and whispered to me that I was NOT to supervise any other tourist's personal shopping, specially clothes, in future.

I'm having a great time so far! The U.K. is very landscapey with hedges and stone walls and thatched roof cottages and no advertising along the roads because it's illegal. I'm supposed to be doing an assignment for Miss James on 'Three Important Historical Sites In England' but I never have much time to work at it. There doesn't seem to be any space in between looking at things and taking photos.

Love
Penny

P.S. If you're over at our place next weekend could you please check in my room and make sure Mum hasn't chucked out my mushroom crop like she threatened to? (Box on the left under my bed, better hold your nose while inspecting.)

the brochure from the wool shop.

some black-faced sheep in paddocks with stone walls. (I'm surprised they haven't heard of barbed-wire over here)

WHEN IN INNERLEITHE
PEEBLESSHIRE

visit our

MILL SHO

Mill Shop

Alistair, I wish you'd quit getting into long discussions with people about how many megawatts of power hydro-electric stations produce per hour — didn't you see me trying to <u>signal</u> you in the wool mill?

Listen, while we were in there, I saw Heidi do a VERY dodgy thing. She was in one of the fitting rooms trying on a kilt, and the curtain wasn't closed properly AND—she put her own skirt back on over the kilt and strolled back out to the bus WITHOUT PAYING! Do you think we should tell her mum or your mum about it or what?

Penny — my mark.

what do you mean, women always act peculiar in shops anyhow and not to worry about it? Hmm?
P.

All right, forget about that kilt, but how about this: she's got eight little Scottish Highlander dolls, just like the ones they <u>had</u> at that place where we stopped for lunch, only Heidi <u>wasn't</u> in the queue lining up at the cash register! P.

Sorry. Get back to your old Trade Union book then, but just don't blame me if Heidi gets arrested AND GIVES AUSTRALIA a bad name.
P

Innerleithen

3 monsters doing the Highland Fling!

Dear Mum and Dad

I saw my first ruined castle! It was on an island in the middle of Loch Lomond only the boat pilot of the Bonnie Jean couldn't land there for us to have a close up look, so I had to make do with photos. (They mightn't turn out too well because of water in the camera, it's okay, don't panic, I didn't fall all the way overboard. Just as well I *did* have my sniper jacket with the hood, because that's what Alistair yanked me back on board with.)

Loch Lomond was pretty spectacular, though a bit cold. Alistair and I sat out in the front part of the boat and it was funny how people kept coming out to join us there and carrying on about how bracing the air was. They gulped in dirty big sucks of it, but I noticed they didn't stay out there long. They all rubbed their hands together, shivered, stamped their feet, turned up their collars and dived back inside coughing to get cups of hot coffee. I didn't mind the cold. (Tracksuit pants on under judo pants and my glove-puppet mittens — left hand: cockatoo, right hand: kookaburra.)

I really hated getting off the boat and leaving beautiful Loch Lomond. I was having one last look all by myself when Alistair yelled from the shore so I had to make a jump for it because they'd pulled the gangway back on. A highland toffee went down my throat the wrong way and Alistair had to thump me on the back, but he wasn't all that sympathetic. He says unemployment is very high in Scotland and the local people probably never had any spare money to spend on toffee and have to watch wealthy tourists guzzle it. (He's doing History of Political Movements as an elective this term and his mum keeps saying she wished he'd chosen pottery instead.)

Give Bill a really big hug from me.

Love,

Penny x x X for Bill

P.S. I've posted a parcel home. Had to mail it because the driver complained it was rattling about in the overhead locker like a clan uprising and distracting him. Don't let Dad see what's inside it. He'll find out soon enough.

Dear Aunty Sue

This is a picture of Loch Lomond. Do you known the song about it? Gus, our tour leader, sang us all the verses and it had a really catchy beat so everyone on the bus joined in, even me. I'd never heard it before and thought it was a song about car rallies and describing different routes to get to Scotland, but Gus suddenly stopped singing and told us the 'low' road in that song really means death. The man who wrote it was in prison and due to be executed next morning. Everyone's happy singing voices sort of choked off when Gus told us that. The words seemed sadder and sadder and everyone went really quiet thinking about them and when the whole bus was totally depressed, Gus switched off the microphone and looked triumphant. *Love,*

Penny X

Scotsman Jock with tam-o-shanter

P.S. Could you please ring Mum and tell her she is on *no account* allowed to chuck out my mushroom crop, I invested a lot of money in it plus all those trips back from the dairy with the manure.

ALISTAIR! Heidi's got four (4!!) metal anchor-shaped ash-trays with 'Bonnie Jean' printed on them! (I thought I heard her clanking a bit when we walked back to the bus.) So? Don't you think it's suspect when people carry ashtrays round stashed away in their boots? P.

Hey, Lucy!

I've just had a good idea. You know the way rhododendrons grow wild all over Scotland, why don't you change the name of the girl in your book from Storme Duval to <u>Rhoda Dendron</u>? Or Heather Wild? I've collected some heather to take back and give to my friend Mrs. B.

wild heather for Mrs. B.

AIR MAIL
PAR AVION

Dear Mrs Bettany

Scotland certainly has got a very colourful history. We've been to see a place called Glencoe where a lot of the Clan Macdonald were murdered in their beds by the Campbells. It's a really spooky place and there wouldn't have been anywhere to run out and hide because it's all big dark bare mountains and rocks. (All the mountains in Scotland are called Ben something and the biggest one is Ben Nevis. Alistair said we could start a fashion in Australia when we get back and call our mountains Sam.)

Glencoe pebbles

The people in our bus acted very peculiar at Glencoe, a bit like being in church and as though the massacre had taken place only last week instead of 13 February 1692. (Alistair knew the exact date.) They all stood around and talked in respectful voices and said they couldn't bear looking at such a tragic place for very long. (But I reckon they didn't hang around once they got their photos because they couldn't stand the cold and wanted to nip back into the heated bus!) I picked up two souvenir pebbles from Glencoe which I put in my sporran (it's coming in handy, that sporran, to keep pens and notebooks in). I'll give one of the pebbles to Mrs MacDonald who lives next door to us and one to Jim Campbell who works with Dad. (They can throw them at each other.)

On the way to the Isle of Skye we passed a historic old castle which Gus said dated from the 13th century so everyone used up masses of film taking shots. (Then Gus said the original 13th century castle was destroyed and the one there now was only a copy built in 1932.)

I thought the sea in between the mainland and the Isle of Skye would be just like it sounds in the song 'Speed Bonnie Boat' which Miss James makes us sing in choir practice — a big wild stretch of ocean with a hurricane howling along it. But talk about a disappointment. I don't know why wimpy Bonnie Prince Charlie even *needed* a boat to get there. You could just about dog paddle over there in a couple of seconds, but we went by ferry with the bus. There was a terrific ruined stone tower and I asked Gus what it was and he scratched his head and said it must be new because he was sure it hadn't been there all the other times he'd taken tours to the Isle of Skye. Alistair looked up his brochure and it was a *real* castle built as a lookout for Vikings! (But Gus wouldn't let us go and see through it because of the schedule.) Heidi said she couldn't understand why Vikings would even want to come to such a freezing boring place, or Bonnie Prince Charlie either, for that matter, and she dived into the nearest souvenir shop.

Mrs B., how do you manage a *kleptomaniac*? (I'm pretty sure that's what Heidi is.) Alistair doesn't believe me yet and just thinks she's got plenty of pocket money, but I'm getting worried. Supposing she ends up being arrested and the good name of Australia will be disgraced? And also, she's so efficient at it there won't be many souvenirs left for the next Hi-Fli Tour bus that comes up this way! I stuck to her like toffee in that souvenir shop, and thought maybe she was turning over a new leaf (or more likely didn't see anything much she fancied) because I didn't catch her out.

I bought two terrific little Highland cattle bookends with wide horns like their own TV aerials. Mrs Ross said they were silly things to buy and they'd poke holes in my suitcase. She didn't even crack a smile when I said I'd have trouble getting them through customs, too, because of livestock having to go into quarantine in Australia.

After the Isle of Skye we headed for Loch Ness and I was so excited I was just about hopping out of my red-back spider top. Heidi didn't even bother looking out the bus window. She said she'd already seen the Loch Ness Monster last time she came to Scotland when she was seven, and she'd taken a really good clear photo of it, which she said she has in her suitcase because it's so valuable. (She was too busy to look out the windows, anyhow. She was counting up all these china thimbles painted with heather. And the souvenir shop on the Isle of Skye had thimbles just like them!)

It's been the biggest diappointment of my life not even getting one little glimpse of the Loch Ness Monster, and it's terrible not to have a photo to show Annette Smurton. Even one hump in the water would have been better than nothing at all. When I got back on the bus I asked Heidi if I could have a print copy of *her* photo, and I guess maybe I've been mistaken about Heidi, because she was as nice as anything! She said she'll get a print done for me as soon as we reach our next hotel and pay for it herself. So maybe I've made a mistake about her being an eight-and-a-half year old kleptomaniac, too.

Love, Penny

Is that stripe the monster? Would Annette even see it?

Application Form for Field Membership

There is a minimum age limit for field members of the Loch Ness and Morar Project of 17 years.

NAME(S) (MR, MRS, MISS) Ms Penny Pollard

ADDRESS .... AGE 11

TEL: ....

PREFERRED DATES: First Choice From Sat. .... To Sat. ....

Second Choice From Sat. .... To Sat. ....

13th Lookout for Vikings on the smooth crossing to Isle of Skye.

Do you suffer from a

If yes, please give

....

Have you any exp

....

....

I have read and
£30 per person,

See below.

Ap

DIARY

Our hotel had a nice manager who gave us such a friendly speech of welcome. I presented him with one of my Aussie goodwill gifts (handmade pottery bandicoot with holes poked in the back to stand biros in) and thanked him for giving me the chance to hear Gaelic spoken.

Mrs Ross took me aside and said crossly he hadn't been speaking Gaelic at all and not to poke fun at people's Scottish accents. She also said she knew why he'd been so friendly, it was to take people's minds off how terrible the hotel was with brown coloured water coming out of the taps. She barged down to complain about rust in the pipes, but it turned out the water is always that colour because of peat.

While Mrs R. was having a sort of mini-revolution in the corridor with the other tourists complaining that it wasn't a first-class hotel like the itinerary promised, I went exploring in a pine forest with Alistair and a dog who belonged to the hotel. I threw the dog a pine cone to fetch, but he wouldn't. (Maybe he only spoke Gaelic.) We caught up with Lucy who was out walking with Dudley Fowler trailing along behind and she couldn't shake him off. I wish it had been Barb instead out on that walk with Lucy, but when we got back to the hostel, he was sitting in the foyer talking to Heidi's mum about North Sea oil rigs and how they can withstand huge gale force winds and 200-metre waves. She was hanging on to his every statistic and jingling all her tinkly bangles every time she raised her sherry glass. It's not fair. Lucy's twice as nice and I just wish Barb would start to pay her some attention.

26

I had to go and get changed because Mrs Ross wouldn't let me into the dining room in my red-back top, and there was this envelope slipped under the door with my name on it and a note: 'Real live photo of the one and only Loch Ness Monster taken by Heidi Denver on a bus tour'. I thought it was very kind and thoughtful of Heidi to take the trouble to find a shop and get the print developed so fast. It's not many people who are given an authentic photograph of the Loch Ness Monster, so I ripped open the envelope like a Campbell getting stuck into a Macdonald. I was still staring at the photo when Mrs Ross came up to get changed for dinner.

She looked over my shoulder and said: 'Yes. Well. *Not* a very flattering photo of you, Penny. Always remember when travelling in company that other people might notice you doing things you'd rather they didn't. You should always try to act ladylike. You know that nice little Heidi Denver? You'd never ever catch *her* doing something like this!'

Heidi must have had her camera poised at the ready, just waiting to get the most insulting shot of me she possibly could.

I'd been in the middle of blowing my nose. The bus had gone over a bump and my finger shot through the paper tissue and went one up nostril clear to the knuckle. That's when she'd pressed the shutter.

There's only one thing you can do with a photo like that.

I wrote on the back: 'Picture of me having emergency intra-nasal first-aid oxygen treatment on the high altitude summit of Ben Nevis where I've been rock climbing with the Scottish Commandoes during a military exercise', and posted it off airmail to Annette Smurton.

![St Andrews Golf Course photograph]

St Andrews Golf Course (the patron saint of golf)

Dear Uncle Brian

Here's a picture of St Andrews Golf Course which is the oldest in the whole world. I met a nice old man on the waterfront. (We were walking along there trying to find a café because the one we'd been booked into by Gus our tour leader closed down seventeen months ago). The old man said he'd always wanted to migrate to Australia because of his rheumatism, so I gave him a gift bottle of Dinky Di goanna oil liniment I had in my sporran.

We were all very late getting back on the bus because of everyone wandering all over St Andrews getting lost trying to find somewhere to have lunch.

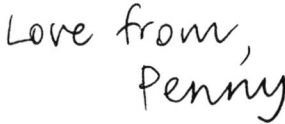

Love from,
Penny

P.S. I got Uncle Dave some tartan golf club protectors in Clan Campbell tartan. (Aunty Sue says he always acts pretty wild when he plays golf and misses a shot.)

Statue of Greyfriars Bobby in Prince's St., Edinburgh

Human watering hole (I wonder if they let dogs in ?)

~~Dear~~ Jason

This little dog statue is in Edinburgh. It's called 'Greyfriars Bobby' and when his master died he sat on the grave for fourteen years and no one could coax him off.

I can't imagine Ferdie sitting on *your* grave for that long, unless it was with a bottle of Scotch whisky to celebrate.

Pollard.

Dear Simone

Here's a picture of a Black Watch sentry guarding the gate at Edinburgh Castle. They stand as still as statues, then turn and march a few steps then turn again and march back and stand at attention and it's like clockwork and neither of them ever misses a beat. (They're certainly a whole lot better than the Kooringa Marching Girls with you dropping the baton all the time and Kylie having to have a bandaid on her left hand so she remembers left from right.)

See ya,
Penny

P.S. There was a sign in Edinburgh Castle saying 'Tattoo Office' but it's a real con. I nicked up there to watch the people getting tattoos and it's only an office where they do all the arrangements for that big military show they have on TV on New Year's Day.

DIARY

There's a pool in this Edinburgh hotel, so Alistair and I went down for a swim, but we weren't quick enough to dodge Heidi. Her bathers are gold and she has matching gold thongs and cap. She looked down her nose at my bathers.

Dudley Fowler was there all by himself. His bathers looked even daggier than mine, as though they'd been buried in silt on the Murray River bed for twenty-five years and he'd hooked them up while fishing. He's so bashful he just said one thing: 'Do you know if Miss Bryson is planning to use the pool before dinner?' I didn't know and he went off to do a few laps of the pool, looking a bit mournful.

Alistair was busy figuring out how the pool filter worked, so I got out and went back upstairs.

The hotel lift's got a very crafty mind tucked away behind its little row of buttons. I pressed 3, but it sailed up to the 5th floor and stopped though there was no one there. Then it shot back down to the basement and its doors snapped open and shut before the people waiting there had time to get in. I pressed 3 again, so it went up to 4 and stopped, but the doors didn't open. I finally coaxed it down to 3 and prised the door ajar to let some people in and myself out.

Mrs Ross was busy getting dressed for the special Night Life Outing where there was going to be a traditional Scottish dinner, Highland dancing, a pipe band and a Scottish comedian, but the itinerary said it was for Adults Only. Mrs Ross said Alistair and I must have our dinner sent up by Room Service

31

because she didn't want us roaming about in a strange hotel while she was out, and we weren't allowed to stay up late, either. Alistair had to go back to his room at 9.30 and I wasn't to sit up writing postcards to people and knitting peculiar things with Australian themes. While she was deciding which of her new tartan outfits to wear, she rattled off more orders such as Alistair and I weren't allowed to play *Get Smart* in the lifts like we did in the first hotel we stayed at, or pretend to be porters and carry luggage up for people hoping for a tip. Then came the worst thing of all — she'd arranged for Heidi to have dinner in our room, too, because Mrs Denver was going on the Night Life Outing as well.

She rang down to the pool with a message that Heidi and Alistair were to come up immediately and told me to knock on Lucy's door and tell her it was time to go. Lucy had been working on *Love Amid The Heather*. She'd got to the part where Storme Duval was having a fight with Douglas Macburnie while out grouse shooting. Lucy was having trouble with his Scottish accent. (It didn't look all that romantic written down, just weird, and she said she might change the setting to Texas and make him a rancher. I pricked up my ears at that.)

I kept the lift doors wedged open with a pot plant while she and Mrs Ross got in and Alistair got out. They pressed the ground floor button, but the lift shot up to the 8th floor and Alistair and I went back to the room feeling a bit left out, like Cinderella.

Heidi took ages to turn up. I thought that maybe she was doing all the rooms over while everyone was out making galahs of themselves dancing Scottish reels, but she'd just been changing. She'd changed from her bathers into a daggy green dress with fringes all over and a pair of silver sandals which she said came from Los Angeles. (I'd seen them though on a shop counter in Edinburgh that afternoon.)

Alistair rang up Room Service and we ordered fish and chips and layer cake. Heidi ordered venison, just to show off, because it was the most expensive thing on the menu. I don't think she really liked it either. She ate only a little bit, then said she was dieting because she didn't want to get fat, looking sideways at me when she said that. I finished dinner and got on with sorting out all my new U.K. badges. Heidi said she'd stopped collecting badges when she was five, then she said she was bored and how about going down to the foyer and sitting around the bar?

Alistair pointed out we weren't allowed to leave the room. I said Heidi could go if she really wanted to, and maybe they'd think she was a garnish and pop her into somebody's drink down in the bar. (The more I looked at her green fringy dress, the more it looked like something out of a salad.) Heidi got in a temper and said I was very juvenile for my age as well as overweight, and she was going down to order an alcoholic drink called Sudden Death and we could just sit there sucking our thumbs and watching TV, then she slammed out.

Alistair and I watched through the door, but all she did was bang the lift door noisily as though she'd gotten in, then she tiptoed back along the corridor to her room, yawning her head off as though it was past her bedtime. So we made ourselves venison sandwiches and cocoa and watched a soccer match replay.

Mrs Ross went mad at us because we were still up when she got back, but she'd brought us back a slice of haggis each.

(I didn't eat mine when I found out how they make it. I put it in my suitcase to take back as a souvenir for Jason Taylor.)

Al,

she just denied it and says she'll sue you for defamation of character. I told her it won't stand up in court because she hasn't got any (character, that is).

Hey Penny,

You might be right about Miss H.D. I'm missing: 3 postcards of Graham Bell's house

1 pamphlet about Lister (Did you know he was born in Edinburgh & invented Listerine?)

1 Blackwatch tartan cover photo album

1 book about Robbie Burns (poet of the working class)

—all bought at the foyer souvenir shop last night on the way up from the pool. Last seen on the coffee table next to the chair Sudden Death was sitting in!

Stealing from the unemployed is a very serious moral offenc

Alistair

P.S. Could you sort her out? I don't know how to talk to girls who are only eight and a half and who wear eye gunk.

Dear Aunt Winifred

We left Scotland and now we're in the Lake District so I took a photo of Wordsworth's grave for you because you like poetry. It was a bit of a scramble when I took this shot, because there was a big bunch of gravestones and *all* of them said Wordsworth and no one could remember the first name of the famous one. Someone said they knew for a fact it was Robert and someone else said they always thought it was Edgar Allan and someone else said it was Dorothy, but luckily a lady on our bus who's a writer knew it was William.

I guess Wordsworth's a pretty natty name for a writer, do you reckon he made it up, like a pen name? Lucy, the writer on our bus, calls herself Phillida Montgomery on her book covers. I'd rather be called Shakespeare. It's got more zing to it.

Love,
Penny

P.S. Give my regards to ~~Bellow and Roar~~ Brendan and Rachel.

Alistair

It was really nice of the lady from New Zealand to give you a present for taking her suitcase down this morning when Gus said his fibrositis was playing up again. Such a cute little book 'My Trip' on the cover in forget-me-nots and all those little bunnies carrying baskets on the pages, aren't you a lucky bloke?

Maybe you could give it to Jason Taylor next time he goes off on a Scout Jamboree.

I don't think that bunch of people by the roadside were unemployed and starving and begging for handouts. You'RE NUTS. They were just waving to the bus.

The Dodgy Brothers <u>are</u> playing little private bus games. Look at what happened when we passed that tower back there. (You had your nose in a book again and missed it all.) Gus said to have a really good look and try to guess which century the tower was built in. So everyone took heaps of photos thinking maybe it was the oldest Saxon tower in the British Isles, but when we drove on Gus said it was just a water tower built a couple of years ago by the government. (He and J. were laughing their heads off, I saw them in the rear vision mirror

P.

G. & J. ——>
laughing their
heads off!

me?
too!

whoops!
I seem to
have lost
my head

Well, if you won't <u>talk</u> because you're too busy reading, how else am I supposed to communicate? P.

Hey, Alistair, I just thought of a good name for Mr Klyne, you know that tall skinny maths teacher at your school:
AULD LANG KLYNE!

OUCH! That hurt, Alistair!

DIARY

Chester was founded by the Romans in AD 60 which is fairly old and it also has a lot of Tudor buildings as well in the shopping centre, and they're all on different levels with black and white timber verandas. I bought a crystal pendant for Mum. It's lovely and sparkly and the only thing wrong with it is maybe it's a bit too big, though she can always use it as a doorknob instead. I bought a stone hedgehog doorstop for Aunty Sue, though Mrs Ross went mad and said I'll have to pay excess freight when we fly home as it weighs more than all our luggage put together.

At the café where we stopped for lunch I ordered a pot of tea, and a nice old lady in a floral apron behind the counter handed me a knitted cap. It seemed a really friendly way to welcome tourists, to give them a free souvenir soccer cap, so I put in politely on my head to show how grateful I was (even though I don't like lime green and purple stripes). She stared at me as though I'd gone bananas and I soon found out why. The person in front of me in the queue also had a knitted hat that looked the same, but he told me it was to put over his teapot, which was what it was meant for in the first place. I was so embarrassed I grabbed the first thing handy for lunch which was called a Bacon Barm. (I was hoping it might be some ancient Roman recipe made only in Chester, but it turned out to be just a plain ordinary roll with bacon inside.)

I had to share a table with Heidi. (Alistair was out looking for examples of class discrimination he could photograph for his file.) She spread out all the stuff

37

she'd got in Chester when I wasn't looking: three pairs of earrings, four Mars Bars, five model Roman soldiers, two egg whisks, one bottle of perfume and a brass lion door-knocker which looked mossy, as though it might have been prised off someone's front door.

'You seem to have a *lot* of pocket money, Heidi,' I said sternly, like Scotland Yard.

'Oh yes, I get lots and lots of lovely money,' she said airily. 'Not like *some* people. I bet you wish you were me!'

'About as much as I'd fancy being one of those Macdonalds at Glencoe,' I said. 'Heidi Denver, you just listen to me —'

But she just stuck her tongue out and I know there's no way she'll ever take any notice of anything I say. She doesn't even like me, for a start, so I shut up and got stuck into my Bacon Barm instead.

Dear Mrs Norris

We had a quick trip to Wales squeezed in after visiting Chester, and I bought a carved wooden love spoon there for Sandy and Yvonne. The spoons are supposed to be traditional in Wales, but I don't know what you'd use them for, a tea strainer, maybe. If you tried to drink soup with it the soup would just trickle out through the holes. But everyone else was rushing around in Wales buying them, even Alistair, so I thought I'd better, too.

Alistair kept on about what a sad history the Welsh people have and how little babies in nappies were made to go down the mines to haul coal, not to mention canaries and ponies, though all the Welsh people we saw in the villages looked pretty cheerful to me. We drove up on top of a mountain to look at a view that Gus, our tour leader, reckoned was the best view in Great Britain and only Hi-Fli Tours knows about it, but we didn't see any of the view because of all the mist up there.

Love,
Penny

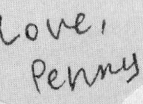

DIARY

Mrs Ross is really annoyed about staying overnight in Liverpool. She says it's just a large ugly industrial city and not a bit landscapey, and she intends writing to the head office of Hi-Fli and telling them how to arrange their itineraries a lot better. She didn't even like the big red chunky cathedral, though I thought it was terrific, something like Ayers Rock with windows.

She held another tourist union meeting over dinner and pointed out all the things promised on the list which didn't happen, e.g. where it said we'd hear a Welsh choir singing traditional Welsh songs but all we got was a crackly bus loudspeaker tape with Gus singing the choruses. And being promised a tour of a Saxon church and then Gus saying what a pity it just happened to be shut that day for a bell ringing rehearsal. (It certainly doesn't look as though the Dodgy Brothers will get a very big tip from anyone at the end of the tour.) Everyone at our table began to grumble and bring up other things such as the promised barge trip along a canal (Gus had claimed it was all silted up with clay). And not being allowed to stop at as many souvenir shops as everyone would like.

Dudley Fowler didn't join in the grumbling. He seems perfectly satisfied with everything and meekly got on with eating the plate of crumbed whiting plonked down in front of him even though he'd ordered roast lamb.

◄ The wonderful view from our London hotel

A collection of stuff of historical interest ► for Miss James

◄ Pets cemetry in Edinburgh

Churchill's and Mrs. Churchill's grave. ►

◄ Emu feet sock finally finishe

Red-back spide windcheater ants pants an Aussie mittens (glove puppets

Me in
souvenirs:
busby, cards,
sporran,
scarves,
umbrella.

Lucy's
tartan

Bill unpacks
his lion from
Harrods!

Barb said he was planning his own itinerary this evening and going out to an English pub to play darts and drink some real English beer even though he'd heard it tasted like boiled aftershave lotion, and who was game enough to come with him? He looked at Lucy, but she said she'd already arranged with someone to go to a choral service at the Ayers Rock cathedral (!).

I rang up Mum and Dad even though it was two o'clock in the morning in Australia, but they didn't mind. Dad asked if we'd seen Stonehenge yet, and I explained Stonehenge wasn't for a couple of days because at the start of the tour Gus announced that due to some unfortunate hotel overbooking, we'd be going around the U.K. back to front from what it had said on the itinerary. They sounded really pleased I'd rung and even got Bill up and let him do one of his spitty yodels into the phone, and when I hung up I felt this stupid lump in my throat like I got at Loch Lomond, only this time it wasn't toffee. It wouldn't go away, so I had to stay in the phone cubicle pretending to dial an overseas business call.

While I was in there pretending to speak Japanese because the desk staff was frowning at me for taking so long, Lucy came down all dressed up for her church service. She looked bright and different, because she was finally wearing her zappy new kilt. She looked really nice, though it seemed a waste because of that Dudley Fowler tagging along behind her like a car trailer.

I could hit her! Just because no one else on the bus talks to Dudley Fowler (he's so boring), Lucy carries on being so careful not to hurt his feelings. She should be a social worker instead of a romantic novelist.

42

SHAKESPEARE
(writer)

William Shakespeare was born in a place called Stratford-on-Avon and his girlfriend lived in an old run-down house called Anne Hathaway's Cottage which I just visited. There are some interesting historical antiques in her house including a table which has a swivel top. When you see visitors coming up the path lined with lavender bushes, you can quickly turn over the rough top of the table (which you'd use for chopping vegetables) to the smooth polished side to show off. (I guess that's where that saying 'turning the tables on someone' comes from.)

There's also a bench where Shakespeare used to sit when he came calling, but it looked pretty uncomfortable to me. If I'd been him I would have arranged to meet Anne Hathaway in town instead. The rest of the house was fantastic, though batty, with uneven floors and rooms added on any old way. (I don't think they bothered much about council permits in those days.)

In one of the souvenir shops in the cottage I bought this postcard of W. Shakespeare

<u>Interesting Fact</u>
He had one ear pierced and a gold sleeper. (I didn't know they went in for ear piercing that far back.)

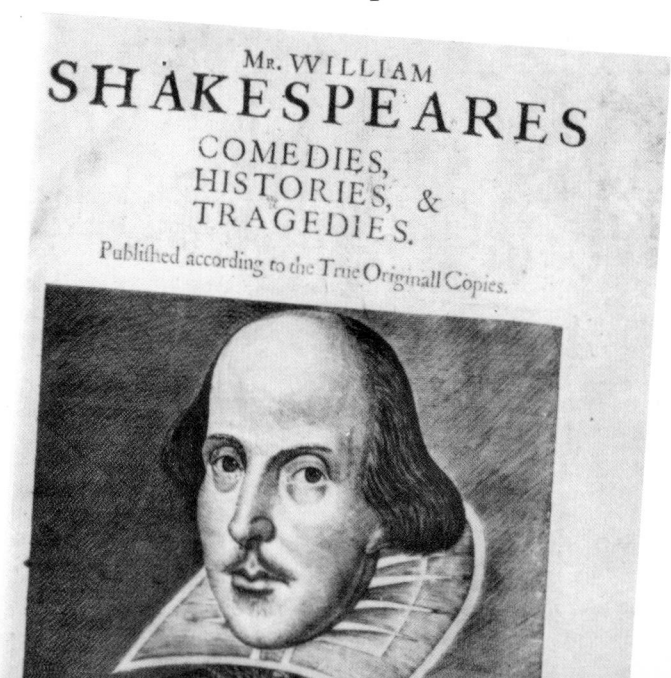

MR. WILLIAM
SHAKESPEARES
COMEDIES,
HISTORIES, &
TRAGEDIES.
Published according to the True Originall Copies.

I also saw the school where he went though he probably didn't like it very much because kids in those days had to go to school from 6 a.m. till 6 p.m. And I certainly can't imagine how I'd get through twelve hours straight of rotten old school! I would have liked to go into that dangerous-looking hiccupy building just in case Shakespeare had carved some brainy graffiti on his desk, but there was a sign up saying No Visitors Allowed In Term Time. Even though I had unbuttoned my jacket so they could see my Aussie flag windcheater and maybe take pity on me because I'd come all the way from Australia, that sign definitely meant what it said. Kids came out every now and then but they didn't take any notice of all the tourists craning over the front gate; I guess they're used to it. (Tourists don't do that at Kooringa P.S., they're always too busy dodging footballs and Jason Taylor.)

I also went to the church where Shakespeare was buried and there were more tourists all standing there with very holy faces looking down at this slab with his name carved on it. I thought I'd better do the same seeing they charged more money to go behind the rope to look at it, but I reckon they could have given him a fancier gravestone. (Like that terrific speckly marble one with the flying angels in Kooringa Cemetery they put up when Mr Farrini died last year.)

Outside in the churchyard I picked up a pebble just in case Shakespeare had touched it, even though Alistair Ross said they probably have tip-trucks coming along to dump loads of new pebbles at the start of each tourist season for gullible people like me. But the one I picked up looks quite old and though the odds are pretty long, maybe Shakespeare had once chucked it at a kid he didn't like from his school.

the pebble Shakespeare might've kicked or thrown or

I also walked along the river Avon where S. had walked making up poems and plays, only I didn't think it would be peaceful enough for him to do that now. It's crowded with tourists and men putting in sewerage pipes and kids practising rowing on the river with their coaches riding bikes along the shore yelling threats and insults. The coaches' insults don't sound as poetic as the ones Shakespeare thought up for his plays. Phillida Montgomery, a famous writer on our bus, let me look through her *Collected Works of Shakespeare* she bought as a souvenir at Anne Hathaway's Cottage, and I found these threats and insults:

1 Turn thee, Benvolio, look upon thy death! (20th century translation: You chicken or something?)
2 Have at thee, coward! (Take that, you wimp!)
3 The devil himself could not pronounce a title more hateful to mine ear! (You give me the irrits, Jason Taylor, and so does the sound of your name!)
4 Thou liest, abhorred tyrant! (It's not fair, you said I could stay up and watch that late movie!)
5 (a) You stubborn ancient knave, you reverent braggart!
5 (b) O inhuman dog! (Both general purpose insults.)
6 What bloody man is that? (Sounds really modern.)

We are staying at this really old hotel in Stratford, so maybe it's one where Shakespeare used to pop in for a beer after work and I might get to see his ghost. That's one very disappointing thing about England. I thought every building over here was supposed to be riddled with ghosts, but I haven't seen even one yet — just Alistair dressed up in a sheet hooting in our window and his mum went mad at him for going out on the fire escape at midnight.
We had to mind Heidi in the shopping centre this

afternoon while Mrs Ross and Mrs Denver went off to have their hair done. She ducked in and out of shops so fast it was like keeping tabs on a lemming! We finally tracked her down and found her with her nose pressed against a jeweller's shop window and a definite gleam in her eye. I felt like flattening her like a brass rubbing, but got interested in the shop window display myself. There was this fabulous ring, like something you could press in sealing wax for important secret documents and the label said it was only five pounds. That didn't seem much to pay for an incredible ring King Henry 8th might have owned, so I went in and asked to try it on. (I decided I just might be able to afford it if I didn't send any more postcards to Annette Smurton from every place we stopped at for morning tea, lunch, afternoon tea and dinner just to show off.)

But when the lady was about to wrap up the ring, I saw the label properly and it wasn't five pounds at all, it was *fifty*! Talk about embarrassing. I had to think fast. I told her I'd just remembered my allergy to metal objects and the reason I was in the U.K. was to consult a top Harley Street specialist because my finger might shrivel up and drop off if I ever wore anything metal (and that I also had to get treatment for my sudden fits of memory loss). I said I was sorry I'd troubled her for nothing. But I could see by her expression she didn't believe me and thought I'd just been mucking about, so I dragged Alistair and Heidi quickly out of the shop. It was two blocks before my face stopped looking like a red traffic light.

Alistair said never mind because only bloated aristocrats on their way to the guillotine wore expensive rings anyhow. I pretended I wasn't disappointed and said I was glad I hadn't been able to afford that ring because it was too heavy, and I'd have ended up with one arm looking like King Kong's. I certainly didn't want bratty little Heidi Denver knowing that I cared, so I hummed cheerfully all the way back to the hotel (just like Simone does on Monday mornings at school and makes everyone sick).

While I was buying a postcard of the River Avon at the foyer desk the receptionist suddenly gave me two free tickets to a play by Shakespeare which is on at a theatre tonight. She said they were by courtesy of the hotel and I was the lucky guest to get them this week. So I went straight upstairs and knocked on Barb's door and gave him those tickets. I said I was sure he'd find some other person on the bus who was travelling all alone like him and who'd just love to go and see a genuine Shakespearean play in Shakespeare's home town.

Lucy came down to dinner with her hair done up in a fancy way, and Barb looked very smart, too, in a suit and tie. I really enjoyed dinner, thinking of how I'd be asked to visit them both in Texas some time in the future when Lucy was Mrs Barber Ziegenhagen.

So I felt really aggro when I saw him go off to the theatre with Mrs Denver! I didn't enjoy the rest of this evening at all! Mrs Ross wouldn't let Alistair and me have a seance to call back Shakespeare's ghost, but I found a little parcel tucked under my pillow when I was just about to get into bed and have an early night. In it was that terrific expensive ring and a note from Heidi saying: 'No trouble at all. Went back and picked it up for you. It wasn't any bother'.

So I had to get dressed again and sneak out of the hotel while Mrs Ross was playing cards in the lounge and find the jeweller's shop and return that ring through the mail slot in the front door. Getting wet in the rain is better than letting Australia be disgraced by a little crook!

STATELY HOMES

Blenheim Palace is the first stately home I've ever seen, not counting my Aunt Winifred's, but it knocks hers for six! Blenheim Palace is where Winston Churchill once lived and it's got a lake in the garden with real islands and also painted ceilings in most of the rooms. (Though I didn't think any of them are as good as the mural I did in my own room of cattle drovers moving a mob of Herefords.)

That big house certainly was spectacular, though Alistair Ross isn't too keen on stately homes. He reckons that the poor servants all died from heart attacks in the olden days because they had to lug sacks of coal up and down stairs and probably had to sleep in cold, rat-infested attics, too, so if they didn't get coronaries, the plague most likely finished them off before their time. But I wouldn't have minded being a servant at Blenheim. You could have had a really great time in the mornings roller-skating around all the long passages before anyone else got up. (But Alistair said even if roller skates had been invented back then, the ruling classes would have kept them a secret for their own use.)

The furniture all had claw feet, and I wouldn't fancy walking there in the dark in case they all turned nasty. Alistair said the cost of just one of those carved chairs would have paid the medical bills to cure all the starving mill workers' children of TB. The guide kept giving him very greasy looks and his mum walked on ahead so people wouldn't think she was related to him.

In one room there were some things Winston Churchill had owned, including his dressing-gown and slippers. I'd feel embarrassed if I became famous and people turned my bedroom into a tourist attraction, especially as I made my slippers out of an old fur stole and cut out two left soles by mistake.

It was a bit confusing listening to the guide talking about Churchill. I thought maybe he was a famous painter as well as being Prime Minister, because she kept pointing out pictures he'd done. In one of the stately rooms she said, 'This is the very last picture Churchill painted before he died above the fireplace'. I was really puzzled and asked her how come Churchill died up there and what was he doing up on a mantelpiece in the first place, but she didn't answer and just frowned at me to shush.

On the ceiling of the front porch at Blenheim there are huge eyes painted to stare down at callers. I don't know if Churchill put them there or not, but they're probably meant to make people think twice about nicking off with the silver. They seem to work quite well, too.

These eyes were painted in 1772 – and have been staring down ever since!

Dear Yvonne and Sandy

We've just had a tour round the city of Bath. There's a street here called The Royal Crescent which is supposed to be the most beautiful street in the world. Everyone was looking forward to getting out of our bus and strolling up and down the most beautiful street in the world, but when we got to it, the driver whizzed round in a circle at top speed five times as though the bus was a skateboard. He claimed it was so we could have a really good look and not miss anything (but I think he was playing a little game he made up). When he stopped everyone staggered out looking the colour of pickles to take photos of the terrace houses. They're really nice, but I found something better to photograph, which was a punk with a terrific hairstyle like spokes on a cartwheel. He was just about to swap a dead glazed blowfly on a pin for my goanna claw keyring which he said would make a great nose stud when Mrs Ross called me away and told me not to get chatting to people like that. Or to give them my address, either (I'd already invited him to stay with us if he ever comes to Australia).

We went on to the incredible old Roman baths and it was peculiar to think about people in togas gossiping on the steps in the olden days before having a swim. Alistair said only *some* people did that because the slaves certainly wouldn't have been allowed to use the pool; they would have all been kept toiling away day and night to cart in enough fuel to keep the water hot.

I wished I could read Latin in case the old stone signs might be saying things like No Running, No Kickboards Allowed, Empty Drink Cans to be Placed in the Bins, and No Distracting the Life Guard on Duty. I asked the guide if you could hire a swimsuit to go in for a dip, but it wasn't allowed, which was disappointing. It would have been tremendous going for a dip in the same water as Julius Caesar!

Love,

Penny x x

P.S. I saw a thatched cottage in a village we went through and it had a dog kennel round the side which had a thatched roof to match! But I guess it wouldn't have impressed Spartacus, he likes his half-galvanized water tank too much.

50

Dear Annette

This is a picture of the very famous ancient Roman baths. I was allowed to have a swim (even though they don't usually let tourists) and found some old Roman coins in the murk at the bottom and also an old buckle which looks as though it's come off a Roman sandal. It's got J. Caesar scratched on it, anyhow.

See ya,
Penny

Penny,
This morning I sprung You-Know-Who in the foyer stuffing two bathmats marked Grand Eastern Hotel into the zip compartment of her suitcase. I took the opportunity of pointing out that she should try to control her undesirable materialistic habits while travelling on an Australian passport. She just said, "What are you talking about?" and kicked me in the shin. Before I could explain further, Mrs Denver came down and said vaguely, "Oh, what a nice kind boy you are, Alistair, helping little Heidi with her luggage. I'm sure you won't mind just running upstairs and fetching mine down, too."

Her luggage, all four (4) pieces of it, is made from ANIMAL SKINS. I gave her some of my pamphlets on anti-vivisection.

Alistair

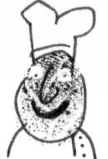

Dear Mrs Bettany

Today we went to Glastonbury which is an old ruined abbey where King Arthur might have been buried. Alistair is nuts about King Arthur even though he doesn't usually approve of the Royalty System, and he took millions of photos around Glastonbury Abbey. (This makes a change from what he's been taking photos of up to now: hydro power stations, reforestation, council housing and air pollution.) While he was lining up an arty shot, I borrowed someone's brown raincoat with a hood and jumped out at him from a stone niche like a monk's ghost. Alistair shot up in the air about a metre, though he pretended he'd only been checking vertical distances for a photograph of the abbot's kitchen. (That little stone kitchen's got a pointy roof like a Kentucky Fried Chicken restaurant. A. said the abbot would turn in his grave if I ever bought it and turned it into a café, especially as I only know how to cook one thing, peanut brittle.)

There's this Dudley Fowler on the bus tour and he kept tagging after Lucy Bryson all over the ruins and even tried to sit next to her on the bus. I came to her rescue and slid quickly into the seat before he could. He must be really getting on poor Lucy's nerves, because although she's not usually snappy, she asked me in a snaky voice not to sing so loudly in time with the sea shanties Gus was playing over the amplifier.

The sea shanties were to get us in the mood for Plymouth Harbour. When we got there, Gus said that he knew a really great waterfront seafood café which was too good to miss, so instead of us buying sandwiches, he'd already taken the liberty of booking the whole group in there for lunch, even though it was a bit expensive. (The owner of the café looked so much like Gus they could have been twin brothers.)

After lunch we went on a harbour cruise and Gus pointed out the steps the Pilgrim Fathers had walked down. All the Americans nearly fell overboard taking pictures, but when we landed they found out Gus had made a mistake and the flight of steps they'd used rolls of film on just led down to a public toilet. He ordered us all to get back on the bus and put on a tape of some music called 'The Cornish Rhapsody' very loud to drown out the mutterings, and we set off on a mini-tour of Cornwall.

I wish you could have seen that fantastic little town in Cornwall! It had steep narrow streets with doors painted bright colours and signs hanging over them, and it looked as though the whole town was on holiday, not just the tourists. (The tourists were all charging into shops to buy brass lanterns and rum keg wastepaper baskets.) There was a man playing a flute on a street corner and he certainly beat Simone Norris. (She only plays two notes then stops to wipe the holes with a pink tissue even if there isn't any spit.) I took off one of my badges which was a cat singing with 'Mewsician' printed underneath and gave it to the flute-player as a reward. Then we had to run like mad for the bus because we'd spent so much time listening to his music.

Love,
Penny X

Ppsst, Alistair, I didn't really get lost. Had to scoot all the way back again and give that man back his flute case. (Heidi said it was a reflex action and she didn't really mean to.)
P.

P.s. Why have you grabbed that seat next to Lucy? She's not all that interested in that book you're planning to write on social injustices.
There are other people on this bus she might like to sit next to.

The Abbot's Kitchen

STONEHENGE

I knew a little bit about Stonehenge even before I saw the real one because once I made a model out of cartons painted grey with a coating of spackle and presented the finished model to the Kooringa Historical Society. It was a shame they couldn't keep it in their club room on permanent display but there wasn't enough room left over for people to attend the meetings.

The real Stonehenge is even bigger, though you aren't allowed to touch the stones, you have to walk along roped-off paths. It's very cold there. Most people weren't just walking, they were galloping to stop their blood freezing solid in the gale force wind that was roaring over Salisbury Plain. Some of them gave up half-way around and just posed for a quick shivery photo then turned and galloped back to their warm buses. But I walked right around because I was really interested in getting material for this assignment. The theory is that Stonehenge is meant to be a calendar only they mysteriously didn't get around to finishing it off.

I don't agree with that theory. No one would be dotty enough to hike across a big cold freezing plain just to find out what the time or the date was. My guess is that it probably wasn't a calendar at all, but a sort of prehistoric football oval. The space inside the stones is small because prehistoric people were a lot shorter. You could have had a really good view from the top of some of the bigger stones, so they were probably intended for rich prehistoric people (like those glassed-in boxes where you are served champagne and oysters at the Melbourne Cricket Ground). You can even see where turnstiles would have fitted in between the spaces, and stone booths where they probably sold footy souvenirs for barrackers to stick on their primitive wagons.

And it's quite easy to figure out why Stonehenge was never finished.

The builders all probably died from pneumonia first.

Dear Alistair,

Before I got back on the bus I bought two hot dogs from the stall (not to eat but to stuff inside my gloves.) When my hands were thawed out enough I checked the pockets of Heidi's gangster coat and sure enough, I found <u>three</u> Stonehenge souvenir spoons. I made her put them back on the counter, even though she said she only took them for something to do to keep warm.

Penny.

P.S. Can't you get Dudley Fowler to sit next to <u>you</u> instead of Lucy and talk to him about cameras?

Never mind the reason! Geeze blokes are <u>dense</u>.
P.

DIARY

Our last day of the bus tour! I can't believe it's over, though we've still got tomorrow for seeing London on our own. I nearly had the chance to visit a place where Iron Age people, Romans, Vikings, Saxons and Normans had *all* lived. Gus told us we'd be passing it, and I couldn't believe our luck, having all that rolled into one and the only thing missing was Shakespeare! But it turned out that all traces of civilization had vanished and they'd moved the town site to some place else. Gus said we'd go straight on and have a quick look at Salisbury Cathedral as a special favour instead. He and Jeffrey were being very smarmy to everyone on this last day of the tour (probably because it was getting close to tipping time). They both made a sloppy speech over the loudspeaker and said we were without doubt the loveliest bunch of tourists they'd ever had the pleasure of escorting around Great Britain, and when we got to Salisbury they even helped everyone tenderly down from the bus, including Dudley Fowler!

Salisbury Cathedral has the highest church spire in England, and they aren't telling lies, either, because when I was lining up my photo I couldn't manage to fit the whole lot in. In the cathedral souvenir shop I bought a brass rubbing of a dead knight in full armour with his feet resting on a little dog. (It will go like bacon and eggs next to the picture I painted for Aunt Winifred's birthday, which is Ned Kelly in *his* armour with a blue heeler. But I don't think blue heelers would let you use them for a foot cushion.) The best thing I liked in that church was a little carving of two angels. One was playing a violin

Salisbury cathedral in two photos
(so I could get the spire in)

and looking very happy, while the other angel didn't look happy at all, as though it wanted to cover its ears.

Gus didn't give us much time to look at that old cathedral. He said he was only thinking of our comfort, as he was sure we'd all want to avoid the heavy peak hour traffic and get back to London early instead of 5 p.m. as it said on the itinerary. As we got nearer London, rain started to drizzle down and all the bus windows fogged up. I suddenly felt very sad looking around at all the people I'd been travelling with. Apart from Lucy and the Denvers who were staying at our London hotel overnight, I'll probably never see any of them ever again. In spite of all the little address books being handed around and people promising faithfully to write to each other, I don't think they will. When you meet new people on holidays you always say you'll keep in touch, but when you get home they don't seem part of your world any more and you forget. It's a pity, really, because it would be ace if everyone in the world knew everyone else and wrote to each other and remembered each other's birthdays.

One of the hardest things was knowing I'd failed with Lucy and Barb. They weren't even sitting next to each other on the last day. (Dudley Fowler had bailed poor Lucy up one last time and was showing her photos of the new fencing he'd put in on his farm.) So I hadn't even been able to help her have a true-life romance of her own. Tomorrow she'll be flying back to Melbourne to her little flat which she says she hates. She'd have looked okay in a Stetson hat, and I'd really been looking forward to visiting her and Barb in Texas. It all seems a terrible waste.

Gus said he hoped we'd all enjoyed the fascinating historical things he'd been going out of his way to show us over the past few days with no overtime salary, either, and added that the bit in the brochure which said we'd be dropped off at our individual hotels was a printing error and meant only for tours of disabled people. In our case we'd all be dropped off at Hyde Park Corner where we could easily get a taxi or bus back to our hotels. He said that if it was left to him and Jeffrey, we most certainly would be delivered right to our front doors, especially as it was raining so hard, but he'd get the sack if he departed from Hi-Fli company rules, and he had six children to support plus an elderly invalid father with emphysema.

It was really awful and final having to say goodbye to everyone at Hyde Park Corner, and what was most depressing of all was that Barb didn't even look sorry to be saying goodbye to Lucy. He just said breezily, 'Nice meeting all you folks!' picked up his suitcases, got into a taxi and that was that.

Penny,
Meant to mention this before but never got around to it. You know that guy from Texas—why did you always say his name in that sassy way? His name was Robert E. Ziegenhagen —Bob for short. Some ambassador for Australia you are, mate. He probably thought you were poking fun at his accent all through the tour.
Al.
P.S. And double larks aren't birds either, you dill. He was talking about double locks on the river.

TOWER OF LONDON

The Tower of London is the most fantastic place I've ever seen in my whole life. While we were waiting in a queue to get in, I was behind an English kid who was in a school group. He stared at my Aussie-flag windcheater then asked if I was a convict and why wasn't I walking around on my hands because everyone knows Australia is upside down.

I said he obviously didn't know that Australians always hopped around like kangaroos because of the upside-down gravity and everyone hopped to places, even the Queen when she comes for Royal visits.

He pointed out a place down by the river where you could buy lunch refreshments and I thought it was friendly international relationships time, but then he said the speciality of the café was imported wallaby-tail mince specially made for Australian convict tourists who'd been released on parole back to the U.K. So then I pretended to be friendly back and asked if he'd like me to send him a souvenir when I got back to Australia. He greedily wrote down his name and address on a bit of paper before I could change my mind and I put it carefully away in my bag. Then I told him he could expect his live funnel-web spider through the mail in about six weeks.

There was a yeoman at the ticket barrier wearing a fancy black and red uniform with E 11 R on the front and a hat like a bucket turned upside down. He told us he had another uniform he wore on special occasions and it took him one-and-a-half hours to get into it! He had special shoes with red and white rosettes on them, to wear with that other uniform, but he

60

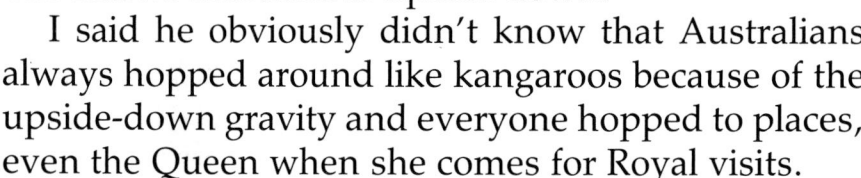

didn't look embarrassed telling us he sometimes wore shoes like that — he looked quite proud!

The first thing we saw was Traitors' Gate. If I'd been a prisoner being hauled in there, I'd have jumped up, grabbed the portcullis, dived over everyone's head and swum like mad underwater back across the river. (It's pretty murky, so there's a fair chance you could have gotten away with it, though maybe they didn't go in for swimming much in the olden days if Bonnie Prince Charlie is any example.)

We went into a tower which was all fitted up as though someone from olden times still lived in it, with a four-poster bed made out of carved oak and curtains you could close like a hospital bed. I had a really good look and when I get home, I'm going to nail some railway sleepers to the corners of my own bed, add a masonite roof and stain the whole lot with brown shoe polish to look like oak.

Then we saw the Crown Jewels, which was like being in the middle of a fireworks display, and then we went into the part where they keep the ancient torture instruments. That kid who'd insulted me about being a convict was in there practically welded to the glass by his eyelids so he wouldn't miss out any grisly details, but I didn't like being in there much and I was glad to get back out into the 20th century and fresh air.

The same kid was in the White Tower which is the best part of the Tower of London because it's where they display all the armour. There was even horse armour, specially made to fit over a horse's head and it was called chanfrons and had two big bumps for the horse's eyeballs. The English kid was taking down excusion notes. I looked over his shoulder and this is what he was writing: 'At the Tower of London I saw some funny looking armour which must have been made especially for a lady'. (!)

Lastly we saw a really old chapel built in 1086 (and you can't get much older than that). It was weird to imagine all the kings and queens who would have stood there, too, maybe on the very same flagstones. (Alistair said the poor underprivileged peasants would have had to stand outside with the rain drenching their rags.) I lay flat on the flagstones to get a really good look at the arches and ceiling, but Mrs Ross made me get up and said I'd give Australia a name worse than Crocodile Dundee. But before I got up I had a strange and fascinating feeling. I felt as though history was standing still and all those centuries were still hanging about under the stone arches like smoke.

And that's why I'm definitely planning to come back to the U.K. one day, because of all the marvellous historical sites I didn't have time to fit in this time around. (Like the 45-year-old petrol pumps in a village I read about and they're still in use!)

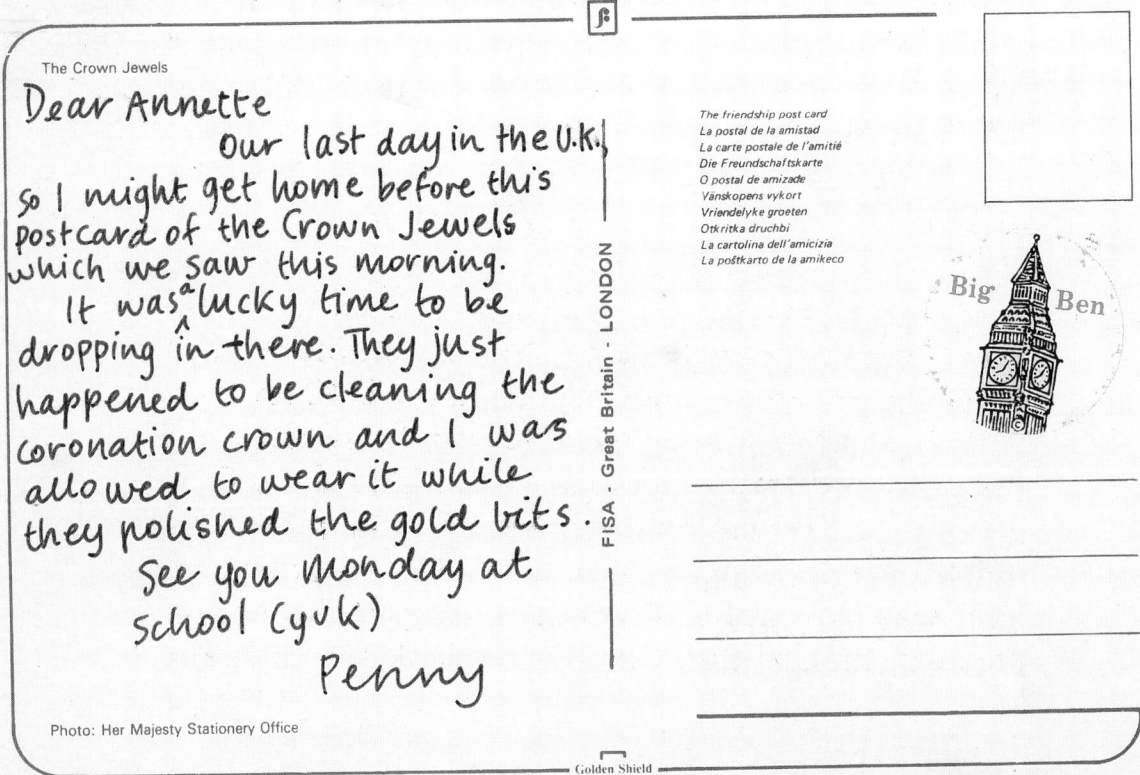

The Crown Jewels

Dear Annette
          Our last day in the U.K.,
so I might get home before this
postcard of the Crown Jewels
which we saw this morning.
    It was a lucky time to be
dropping in there. They just
happened to be cleaning the
coronation crown and I was
allowed to wear it while
they polished the gold bits.
    See you Monday at
school (yuk)
          Penny

The friendship post card
La postal de la amistad
La carte postale de l'amitié
Die Freundschaftskarte
O postal de amizade
Vänskopens vykort
Vriendelyke groeten
Otkritka druchbi
La cartolina dell'amicizia
La poŝtkarto de la amikeco

FISA - Great Britain - LONDON

Big Ben

Photo: Her Majesty Stationery Office

Golden Shield

FISA IG Palaudarius 26 Ben   Printed in the E.E.C

L-62

DIARY

Our last day started with Mrs Ross making me wash and dry my hair even though I'd already done it last night. I'd had this great idea in the middle of the night and wet my hair out of the water jug and plaited it in dozens of tight skinny braids. Then before breakfast I combed it all out into a frizz like a lion's mane. I meant it as a sincere compliment to England because the lion is one of their emblems, but Mrs Ross said it looked more like a declaration of war and made me wash it all out. She wouldn't let me go down to the dining room while it was drying, so I had to have a continental breakfast all by myself in our room. I didn't mind. I was really looking forward to that continental breakfast, thinking it might be a tray loaded with things like stuffed olives, Black Forest cake and pastrami, but it was just two rolls and honey.

Even on our last day we were landed with Heidi! Mrs Denver decided she needed a professional manicure and blonde streaks before nipping over to Canada (which is where they're going next), so Mrs Ross offered to take Heidi sight-seeing with us. Lucy came along, too, and I bet she was heaving a sigh of relief because Dudley Fowler had to go and fix up something about his return tickets. At least she didn't have him tagging along on her last day in the U.K. She was hard to steer in a straight line along the street to the underground station. She kept seeing romantic English things she wanted to photograph like a man in a bowler hat carrying a rolled umbrella, and pigeons. She was in raptures about seeing real London pigeons, though they don't really look any different from Aussie ones. At the station there was even a sign up saying 'Please don't feed the pigeons, they are a health hazard and nuisance'. (Someone had crossed out 'pigeons' and written in 'staff' instead.)

We went to the Tower of London where I bought a surprise souvenir for Lucy. It was a plain gold B on a chain, like the pendant Anne Boleyn (one of King Henry 8th's wives) wore in her portrait. I knew Lucy would like it because she's nuts about history and also because her surname starts with a B. (It would have been better if things had worked out and I'd been able to get her a 'Z' for 'Ziegenhagen' pendant.) Instead I planned to give the Anne Boleyn one to her to cheer her up on the plane going home, because last night she'd been sad at the thought of leaving the U.K. and the closest thing she'd got to hearing nightingales sing were the bird impressions Gus kept doing over the loudspeaker.

Tower B

Tower of London

In the Tower of London.

I'll make Lucy a railway bed of this (should sound s[...] mo[...])

upper Room in the Bloody Tower
(I'm not swearing)

After the Tower of London we only had a couple of hours before we had to leave for the airport, so we had votes about how we'd fill in the time. I really wanted to vote for the mews where they keep the royal horses, but I didn't like to say so because no one else mentioned it. Mrs Ross had things all planned out, anyhow. She said tourists in London *never* missed seeing Westminster Abbey which we could fit in before we went to Harrods where she'd arranged to meet Mrs Denver to hand Heidi back. Heidi was being very quiet for some reason. Mrs Ross said the poor thing was tired, but my guess was that Heidi was quiet just because she was busy making space in all her available pockets for our visit to Harrods.

In Westminster Abbey Lucy went straight to the tomb of the Unknown Soldier and stood gazing at it with a sad face, though I couldn't work out why, as it wasn't as if she'd known him or anything. The tomb I liked best was nearly the same size and shape as a billiard table, which I thought was a brilliant idea. It would be nice to have it in your own living room where all your relations could play billiards — maybe you'd still feel part of things.

We saw the Coronation Chair, too. It was very old and battered because people had carved their initials and dates on it a long time ago. (They had vandals back then, too!) I looked carefully to see if there was any saying E 11 R, but Queen Elizabeth couldn't have been bored at her coronation, or, if she had been, she behaved herself. I could tell Alistair really secretly liked looking at all those old historical things, but every now and then he'd remember his image and say, 'I think all this is degenerate! How come peasants didn't get buried in rich tombs like the ruling

65

class? That gold leaf stuff could have paid some poor peasant's peat bills for a whole year!'

Heidi was getting quieter and quieter and I started to worry that maybe she was coming down with 'flu. Perhaps her mum would decide not to go on to Canada, but come back with us instead and I'd be stuck with Heidi in the plane all the way to Australia! She didn't cheer up even when we got to Harrods, though Mrs Ross went crazy there. She bought herself an English raincoat with a checked lining and a tweedy hat. (Alistair whispered to me that all she needed now was a King Charles spaniel on a leash, a cup of Horlicks and a plate of plovers' eggs.) While she and Lucy were buying last minute gifts of English lavender soap, Alistair and I went up to the toy department. Alistair headed straight for the electronics counter, but I had something very special I wanted to buy in the soft toys section, a super colossal present to take back to Bill. It didn't take very long to find the exact perfect one.

It was the big hairy lion with crossed eyes and flubby paws and a terrific sleepy expression on his face, as though he was full of antelope and wouldn't do any harm to anyone (at least for the time being). I knew Bill would slobber and yodel like mad the moment he set eyes on that lion.

'I never knew you liked stuffed toys,' Heidi said.

I explained that it was for my baby brother and thinking of Bill made me get out the photo Uncle Dave had taken at our dinner table. Though I liked Harrods and the Tower and everything in the U.K., I could suddenly hardly wait to get home and sit down at that table with Bill and Mum and Dad and everyone. Heidi had a good old stickybeak over my shoulder, and I was a bit embarrassed. It isn't the kind of family photo you pass around and show people.

Uncle Dave hadn't even meant to take it, he'd just been showing off with his new camera and accidentally pressed the shutter. It was a pretty weird photo. Bill was reaching out from his high chair with his Mad Dog Morgan face on to tip pureed vegetables over my head. (I can't say I blame him, because I had a taste of them once.) Dad had just got back from footy and still had his barracking cap on with the aeroplane propeller on top. Mum was still in the middle of reading out loud to Dad a poem I'd written about Infinity and they were both falling around laughing their heads off. (I still can't figure out why, as that poem was meant to be dead serious.)

I quickly put the photo away and thought if Heidi said anything about my family and our messy dinner table, I'd really dong her right there in the middle of Harrods, even if it did give Australia a bad name. But she just said, 'You're lucky, Penny, having a cute little baby brother and your mum and dad still together like that and having fun.'

But I couldn't answer because I'd just looked at the price tag on the lion and could have howled from disappointment. As Alistair would have said (if he hadn't had his nose stuck in a build-your-own personal computer kit) that lion cost enough to buy every peasant a Christmas hamper for the next fifty years! It really hurt to have to put it back on the shelf, specially as it flopped over on its back with its paws stuck sadly up in the air as though it really wanted to come to Australia and belong to Bill.

So I'd just have to buy him a plastic Bobby's helmet at the souvenir shop in Heathrow Airport, but it was hard to walk out of the toy department and look back at that terrific lion lying there waiting for someone else to buy him. No one else could possibly like him as much as Bill would have, either!

We all went downstairs to meet Mrs Denver on the ground floor as arranged. Then it was time to say goodbye forever to Heidi. I looked at her and felt pleased because she'd somehow managed to get through the whole of Harrods and not pinch anything, but I couldn't really praise her out aloud in front of her mum for something like that. I looked at her mum standing there with that thin papery smile plastered on her suntan and her cobra eyes. She didn't look one bit like anyone's mother I knew. You certainly couldn't imagine running to her if you'd fallen off the laundry roof and dislocated your shoulder playing Wonderwoman. She'd probably just say, 'Serve you right, you little pest, and don't bawl, either, you'll spoil this new coat of nail varnish I just put on.'

So I took off my best badge and gave it to Heidi, and although I certainly hadn't planned to, I heard myself telling her that when she got back to Australia, she could come over to my place and visit and we'd look through all our tour photos together. Then I turned away and went quickly after Mrs Ross, understanding a bit better why Heidi collected all those pathetic little goodies for herself.

Mrs Ross was in a bit of a snitch. She said huffily, 'Lucy ran into that tedious man from the Murray River, Duncan or Dudley or whatever his name is. It looked to me as though he'd *arranged* to meet her in Harrods. I must say it's very rude of her going off with him to have afternoon tea, and I only hope she gets herself back to the hotel in time for us to leave for the airport.'

She decided (with some helpful nagging from Alistair) that we could just fit in a ride on a double-decker bus before we went back to get our luggage.

We sat upstairs in the front seat and it was a fantastic way to see London. We went through the city and over the Thames, then the bus drove right inside a very old ricketty building with a high roof and the driver switched off the engine. Mrs Ross said the building was probably so antique they had it on the National Heritage List and the bus must drive in there especially for tourists to take photos. She looked around and said maybe it was an old Elizabethan dining hall, so we used up the last of our films taking photos from every possible angle.

Then a bus conductor put his head upstairs and seemed surprised anyone was still on board, because the building was actually the bus depot. So we got into a taxi and headed back for the hotel to collect our luggage. Although we'd seen all those terrific things on our last day, I wished and wished I'd had a chance to see the Royal Mews, but I didn't tell Alistair or Mrs Ross how disappointed I was at missing out on that. Not many kids my age get the chance of travelling all over England and Scotland without having to pay and seeing things like armour made especially for horses. I could buy a postcard of the Changing of the Guard at the hotel desk and not send it to Annette Smurton, but keep it for myself, and it would just have to do. (But it wasn't really the same thing.)

As we got to Hyde Park Corner, our taxi got caught up in a traffic jam and Mrs Ross started to panic, thinking we might miss our flight, even through there was plenty of time.

And right then, something spectacular happened!

A troop of soldiers came riding past all the waiting traffic, in red jackets, gold buttons and tall black furry caps. They were all sitting up straight as candles and the horses were in perfect step. All around us was the

sound of hooves and the jingle of brass and the beautiful smell of horses and leather. It was like having my very own personal Changing of the Guard!

I didn't really mind that I'd used up my last film on a bus depot. Certain things don't need to be photographed, anyhow. You know they'll stick in your memory for ever and ever.

The taxi waited outside our hotel while we went in to collect the luggage, but the receptionist called us over to the desk, because there was a message for Mrs Ross and a parcel addressed to me, all wrapped up in a Harrods bag. There was a note inside saying, 'Dear Penny, see you in Australia when I get back from wherever. Love, Heidi. P.S. I *paid* for this lion out of my pocket money, really and truly. The docket's there to prove it.'

Mrs Ross's note had been left at the desk by Lucy, who'd already called and collected her luggage half an hour ago.

'Oh dear, I knew we shouldn't have gone on that bus ride,' Mrs Ross said. 'Lucy is so vague and not really fit to be wandering all over London by herself. I thought I'd made it plain to her to wait here till we got back and we'd share the same taxi to the airport. To save me getting my reading glasses out, you read this, Penny, and make sure she's headed off in the right direction.'

'Dear Mrs Ross, I've decided to stay on in the U.K. for a few more weeks. I'm sorry I didn't have time to explain this afternoon, but I didn't know my plans then. I never imagined I'd receive a proposal of marriage in such a romantic spot as the travel department of Harrods! When Dudley and I get back to Melbourne to make our wedding arrangements, you and Alistair and Penny will certainly receive invitations. Hope you have a good trip back, love from Lucy Bryson.'

Well!

All I can think of is that B pendant which she won't have any use for now her name's going to be Lucy Fowler!

Still, it won't go to waste.

I know someone else I can give it to instead.

Bobbie's hat

Bill's beaut lion from Harrods with the flubby paws (and fishing-line whiskers!)

Tartan Teddy

Toy double-decker bus.